What people
AN UNINTENTION

"In AN UNINTENTIONAL ACCOMPLICE, Carolyn Baker lulls us through her "cookie cutter" Southern California childhood and Girl Scout "white bred" mantras—that mirror of Disneylandish life—as we bask on the beach in our own smug skins. Then, like a stiletto, she slips in Emmett Till's American tragedy making Klan enablers of us all without any need to dress-up in a great white sheet. Baker has clearly called out racism as the time-less tragedy in our time." ~**Richard L. Mitchell, PhD, Cornell University, author of The Education of Adult Offenders**

"By honoring the process of reflection, Carolyn Baker faces her status as a privileged white woman growing up in the United States in AN UNINTENTIONAL ACCOM-PLICE. Her examination of the implicit/explicit racism deeply rooted in our culture leads her to acknowledge her own racial biases. White Americans are encouraged to follow her lead in the hopes of getting to a place of truth and reconciliation in our country." ~**Emily Scott, Financial Guide and Thought Partner**

"Carolyn Baker's AN UNINTENTIONAL ACCOMPLICE is a deeply moving example of what a heart opened to the suffering of others can inspire." ~**Amber Jayanti, founder of the International School for Tarot & Qaba-lah Study, 1975, Code Pink Activist since 2006**

"The true story of one woman's personal journey towards life-changing discoveries about white privilege and race. In AN UNINTENTIONAL ACCOMPLICE, Car-olyn Baker's realizations are told with gentle eloquence and deliver enlightening perspectives and compelling insights with power and conviction. Her conclusions ring true, and the importance of Baker's message is all the more real and urgent as she offers a new holistic and collaborative approach to understanding and overcoming racism." **~The Honorable John Ladner, Los Angeles Superior Court Commissioner, retired**

"A deep an insightful exploration of personal awakening from the heart of white privilege. AN UNINTENTIONAL ACCOMPLICE leads the reader to their own historical truths that have designed and shaped the hidden societal norms of racism . An honest discovery that shines light on the shadow of division in America to support a needed shift in consciousness and a greater healing of humanity." **~Lauren Monroe, Healing artist, speaker and co-founder of Project Resiliency and Mind Body Drum**

AN UNINTENTIONAL
ACCOMPLICE

AN UNINTENTIONAL ACCOMPLICE

A PERSONAL PERSPECTIVE ON WHITE RESPONSIBILITY

CAROLYN L. BAKER

Introduction by Gabrielle David

FLORIDA ■ NEW YORK
www.2leafpress.org

P.O. Box 4378
Grand Central Station
New York, New York 10163-4378
editor@2leafpress.org
www.2leafpress.org

2LEAF PRESS INC. is a
Florida-based nonprofit 501(c)(3)
organization that promotes
multicultural literature and literacy.
www.2lpinc.org

Library of Congress Control Number: 2019930234
ISBN-13: 978-1-940939-23-0 (Paperback)
ISBN-13: 978-1-7346181-2-9 (eBook)

10   9   8   7   6   5   4   3   2   1

Published in the United States of America

First Edition | First Printing

2Leaf Press trade distribution is handled by University of Chicago Press / Chicago Distribution Center (www.press.uchicago.edu) 773.702.7010. Titles are also available for corporate, premium, and special sales. Please direct inquiries to the UCP Sales Department, 773.702.7248.

To my siblings Barbara, Stan, and John
To the memory of our parents
Earl and Mary Louise Baker
And to my children Jaime and Samuel
and my grandchildren.

CONTENTS

PREFACE

AN UNINTENTIONAL ACCOMPLICE: *A Personal Perspective on White Responsibility* goes beyond memoir to my observations on complex twenty-first century social issues such as race and class struggles, identity politics, and feminism. The eight chapters of this book are organized to chronicle my intellectual and emotional development, and consciousness-raising, which parallels the transformative social movements of the sixties generation.

My initial purpose in sitting down to write was to overcome "career whiplash" after exiting a thirty-year career in the nonprofit sector, and facing the great unknown. Writing had been a large part of my job description, but it was technical writing from my head rather than my heart. My original goal was to explore and process a collection of my professional observations and evaluations. How the writing evolved from there is a story unto itself. I started writing on November 1, 2018, as part of the annual National Novel Writing Month, with a commitment to writing 50,000 words by November 30, 2018. This global online community supports authors carving out time each day to write. Not to edit, not to research, not to revise. Just to write. Every November for five years, I'd written drafts of historical fiction novels based on the imagined lives of my white pioneer ancestors. These stories are my heritage, the people from which I came. It was through this fictional writing process that questions about my white identity were being worked out by my characters. For example, how my great and second great-grandmothers felt, following their men at great peril and loss. Or how the Quakers dealt with their moral dilemmas, such as the genocide of Native Americans and the Civil War.

As I started writing in 2018, the topics accelerated into deeper and deeper territory concerning present day race and class distinctions. As I began to describe my personal "aha" moments, I found myself both a witness and a participant, both the prosecution and the defense. I found I was writing about what I needed to understand. Perspectives on how I was socialized began to shift in both subtle and powerful ways. I started questioning notions I held of the American narrative, as well as my own. Reviewing my evolution, and that of American culture, made me realize how little I knew, or possibly even cared, about individuals with lived experience other than my own. By November 30, a rough draft of *An Unintentional Accomplice* was mostly finished. I'm indebted to Gabrielle David, publisher of 2Leaf Press, who took an interest in the manuscript and directed me to frame-changing resources that allowed me to dig deeper into my story. Through interactions with Gabrielle it became clearer to me why I was writing this book, and why now.

So, when people ask me how long did it took me to write *An Unintentional Accomplice,* I'm tempted to say "my whole life," as the chapters reflect the six and a half decades I have lived thus far. This book offers a non-judgmental narrative that invites readers to explore the complexities of race in America and how to navigate the guilt that can arise in the face of these realities. I wanted to illustrate the distance between the American dream and American reality, and suggest relevant ways to change direction.

When reading this book I hope people like me, and perhaps those unlike me, can examine deeply held, and quite possibly unquestioned, racial viewpoints and responses. I encourage readers to be more open-minded and less sure of their position. From writing this book I've realized the importance of breaking the code of white silence and indifference. Many more stories such as mine and honest conversations among white people are needed. So with these eight chapters I add my account, with all its missteps, mistakes, and lack of insight. After reading this book, I would like readers to keenly recognize and call out race and class discrimination when they see it.

My exploration of whiteness continues. Hopefully, my discoveries are making me a better citizen, parent, and friend. Developing the book from a thought in my head to the book in your hands was a very timely and personal process, which has shifted me towards listening with an open heart and mind, and with understanding as the goal rather than gaining the advantage, or being right. May my story serve to help acknowledge pain, reckon history, and lead toward liberty and justice for all. ■

— Carolyn L. Baker
Los Angeles, CA

INTRODUCTION: HIDING IN PLAIN SIGHT

W HEN CAROLYN BAKER contacted me about publishing her book, I was intrigued. Part of 2Leaf Press' mandate is to publish works that challenge race and gender issues in America. While much of our narrative work appears under our 2LP EXPLORATIONS IN DIVERSITY series, we have begun to publish memoirs and personal narratives outside of the series as well. When she explained to me the premise of her book was based on her learning about Emmett Till for the first time in her early-sixties, I decided to take her on.

An Unintentional Accomplice, A Personal Perspective on White Responsibility is Baker's memoiristic journey of rediscovery as it pertains to whiteness, its implications, and impact on her life. She talks about what it was like growing up as a white woman in a working-class neighborhood in Los Angeles during the 1950s and 1960s, and years later coming to terms with the complexity of racism. During her life, she never gave much thought to racism, even though she encountered first-hand racial tension. But it was when Baker learned about Emmett Till that she began to question her long-held assumptions about race and white privilege.

Her approach in writing *An Unintentional Accomplice* was to share her relatable lived experiences and focus on how the effects of racism have shaped her life to an extent so profoundly that she could not see the ways she was the recipient of white privilege and its benefits. She reveals how her views on race have evolved on both a conscious and unconscious level, and what that process has meant for her. Even though Baker never outwardly disparaged people of color, and lived a religious-based lifestyle geared toward nonprofit efficacy, the effects of racism was a central force in her life. By addressing her own internal biases, Baker wanted to set an example that would hopefully elicit conversations about race by talking openly about issues like white privilege, the legacy of racism, and how diversity makes us all stronger.

Like all black women, I live with the historical roots of slavery and the intersectionality of being black and a woman. Black people have always been forced to carry the burden of racial oppression, even though we are not responsible for creating the racial construct we are deigned to live in. In order to have survived all these centuries, black people have learned to understand white people better than they know themselves. We know that racism is not just an attitude or a feeling toward people who are different than you; racism is part of a structural, institutional system that has benefited white people from the day Europeans landed on this soil. Subsequently, they control the political, judicial, educational, health, and legal systems. Most white people find this hard to accept.

Some would suggest that it is the systems that are broken. But none of these systems are broken; it is white people who are broken, but they do not have to be. And broken is not evil. Broken means it can be fixed. Healed. Changed. And recently, quite a few white people are stepping up to acknowledge, repair, and heal. This is what Baker has set out to do, to understand a complicated American structure that holds us all hostage. It was clear she needed someone like me to help her, an African American woman, so I decided to publish this book. I did it because I believe it is important to talk about race from the perspective of both white people and people of color so that we can learn from one another. I also did it because I believe in Baker's motives and her desire for change. As Baker fine-tuned this book, my only input was to push her to be completely honest and dig further, knowing she might see some things about herself that will make her uncomfortable and cringe. Only then would readers be able to connect to her stories and her authentic-self, from the heart.

* * *

THE MURDER OF EMMETT TILL is remembered as one of the most hideous hate crimes of the twentieth century, a brutal episode in American history that helped kindle the civil rights movement. But as far as African Americans are concerned, for every Emmett Till story, there are hundreds more we will never know. Still, I was not surprised by Baker's confession about not knowing about Emmett until six decades later. White people's perception of American history contains few people of color, which is why so many of them are convinced that America is a "white country." That is part of it. The other part is that white people live isolated lives (this does not include the occasional interaction with people of color), and know little to nothing about black people except what is spoon-fed to them by the media and a few mentions in a history book. As she shares her life story, Baker points this out and reaffirms this throughout her book. This systemic and institutional control allows white people to live in a social and cultural environment that protects and insulates them from the whole of American society.

For those who are not familiar, Emmett Till was a fourteen-year-old Chicago boy who went to Mississippi in the summer of 1955 to visit family. In the tiny Delta town of Money, he allegedly whistled or made some suggestive remark to Carolyn Bryant, a white woman at the grocery store. Over the years, the stories would keep changing. She told her husband, Roy Bryant, and with his half-brother, J.W. Milam and probably others, kidnapped, beaten, tortured, mutilated and shot Emmett. Then they weighed his body down with a cotton gin fan by tying it with barbed wire and threw him into the Tallahatchie River. After Emmett's body was discovered, the brothers were questioned and brought to trial before an all-white jury that acquitted them. Then, for a few thousand dollars, the murderers confessed their crime in a 1956 interview with *Look* magazine, and still, nothing was done.

In recent years, Emmett has been the subject of documentaries, films, books, plays, and poems. He is prominently featured and memorialized in The National Museum of African American History and Culture (Smithsonian Institution) on the National Mall in Washington, D.C. An Emmett Till Memorial Commission was established in 2006. The Sumner County Courthouse, where the brothers' trial was held, was restored and houses the Emmett Till Interpretive Center. Fifty-one sites in the

Mississippi Delta have memorialized Emmett. Memorials have the power to invite meaningful race conversations, but the key is addressing stubborn attitudes, stereotypes, and assumptions that have been hardened and passed down over generations. The difficulty is getting beyond feelings of recrimination and guilt.

It is probably why the Emmett Till story will never escape black America's consciousness. When we look at Emmett today, we know that if a white boy walked down the street with a bag of Skittles and a can of Arizona iced tea wearing a hoodie, his whiteness would protect him from being shot. We know why white people did not stand up for Trayvon Martin because, in their orbit, no white boy would ever get shot for just walking down the street. Instead, white people rationalized and quickly concluded that while Trayvon's murder is tragic, he must have done something to perpetuate it. And even if that "something" was misconstrued, he should have known better and bears some responsibility for his death, steering full responsibility away from the shooter. Trayvon's blackness killed him, the same blackness that killed Emmett. A "stand your ground" law that allows white people to claim that fear made them do it, killed Trayvon; while an old-fashioned lynching killed Emmett. It is why Emmett still resonates today. It is why, after all these years, when Baker stumbled upon Emmett and his legacy, not only did she see the ugliness of racism up close for the very first time, she empathized with Emmett's mother, Mamie Till-Mobley, as a mother who also has a son. Sometimes an unbearable event connects us, despite our cultural differences.

An Unintentional Accomplice is not meant to be redemptive, nor was it written to prove that Baker is a bad white person who has finally seen the light, or that other white people are bad because they may not consider her viewpoint. It is her story, and in the telling, she shares the realization that things were never what they appeared to be. That Emmett Till triggered her story, makes it more meaningful. Yet, some black people may read this book, shrug their shoulders and dismiss her words as nothing more than the obvious truth that has been staring her in the face her entire life. On the other hand, some white people will say that Baker is feeding into self-hatred to become one of "them." A traitor to the race. Or making a big deal over nothing and stirring the pot. This kind of back and forth seems to be everywhere, from intellectuals arguing in books and essays to the general public arguing on social media. White people are tired of being called racists, while black people are tired of white people being in denial. Making racist remarks or having racist ideas is paradoxical. Even if you know in your heart that you are not racist, it is possible to have implicit or unconscious racial biases.

Baker understands that there is no magic wand to wave all of this away, and that she along with other white people will never be "cured" from racism and white privilege, but acknowledging its existence and rising to the challenge is the first big step in front of a long road ahead. Overcoming bias is a long-term process that requires sustained work that Baker has embarked on and is committed to do.

Sixty years later, Emmett Till is still with us. In 2004, the U.S. Department of Justice (DOJ) halfheartedly reopened the case to determine whether anyone other than Bryant and Milam was involved. After exhuming Emmett's body, in 2007, the grand jury failed to find sufficient cause for charges against Carolyn Bryant. In 2017, author Timothy

Tyson released details of a 2008 interview with Bryant, during which she disclosed that she had fabricated the most sensational part of her testimony. It also raises the question of why no one was brought to justice in the most notorious racially-motivated murder of the twentieth century. In a report to Congress in 2018, the DOJ stated that it was reopening the investigation into Emmett's murder due to unspecified, new information. But anyone who has studied this case knows that there was always more to it than meets the eye. The cardinal sin is that this benign neglect is so perfectly normal when it comes to black people that Emmett's case will never be fully resolved.

✳ ✳ ✳

Today we are living in a political, social, and cultural moment where open expressions of racial bigotry and intolerance have become more frequent and belligerent. The number of hate crimes and membership in hate groups is increasing. Issues like immigration and crime are being used to incite racial fears among whites. There are no more dog whistles; our leaders are using bullhorns to spread their racism. Racism is so entrenched in American society that most white people are unable to see it or its effects on everyday life, but it is very real and it exists. It has become the primary determinant of human traits and capacities, with racial differences playing an integral role in how we view those we believe are inferior or superior. Some researchers have even argued that more attention should be given to modifying social environments, as opposed to changing the attitudes of individuals.

The campaign against racism has now taken the form of an intra-white conflict. Reverse racism or reverse discrimination has become the mantra with a segment of the white population who believe the social and economic gains by black people in the U.S. have caused disadvantages for white people. They refuse to accept the existence of structural racism and its symptoms as well as the benefits of white privilege. They also believe affirmative action and similar color-conscious programs for redressing racial inequality are a form of anti-white racism, even though there is little to no empirical evidence that white Americans suffer systemic discrimination.

I want to point out that the cost of racism affects white people as much as it affects people of color. It is why real remedies require a frank discussion with white people who are willing to come forward and share their stories. Stories that are imperfect. Stories that might make you cringe. Stories that are real, just like Baker's.

Baker suggests an interpretive strategy directed to the hidden or repressed meanings behind white privilege by questioning and examining its origins. She concludes that white people can and should listen, learn, and speak up, suggesting some steady and even simple steps towards becoming allies in the fight against racism and racial inequity. Sometimes, a simple "I agree" is enough, or better yet, publicly challenging openly racist actions and words. Yet, well-meaning white people get confused about when to speak up and when to shut up, and they are terrified of saying or doing the wrong thing, but inaction is not a solution. In addition to the checklist Baker provides at the end of the book, she also suggests to white readers they should reassess their lives as she has done, and use their lived experiences as a benchmark to move forward.

We can no longer afford to ignore racism. Americans need to find ways to come together and be active in their efforts to confront and combat racist thinking, including their own. Reading books, essays, and research may be helpful, but in the end, it is what is in the heart that truly determines how people will proceed. Carolyn Baker has taken the first step, from the heart. I hope that *An Unintentional Accomplice* will provoke others to do the same.■

— Gabrielle David
New York, NY

CHAPTER 1

GROWING UP IN SEGREGATED SOUTHERN CALIFORNIA

"A true revolution of values will soon cause us to question the fairness and justice of many of our past and present policies." —**Dr. Martin Luther King Jr.**

I AM A BLUE-EYED WHITE WOMAN, part of the baby boomer generation, and the proud daughter of a thirty-three-year Navy Veteran. I grew up during the 1950s and 1960s in Lakewood, California, "Tomorrow's City Today," the most extensive planned suburb in postwar America. Within Lakewood is a group of 444 homes known as Lakewood Gardens, and its Lakewood Gardens Civic Association, the oldest California homeowners' association in operation since 1948. The story of Lakewood Gardens is the quintessential story of post-World War II life in sunny Southern California. To understand life in Lakewood Gardens is to understand how residential and economic segregation was sanctioned in California during that era.

My story begins with my father, Lieutenant Commander Earl Ross Baker, whom I adored, and the Serviceman's Readjustment Act, better known as the GI Bill. The Veterans Administration provided servicemen and women, such as my father, with low-interest mortgages to purchase homes in the post-war era. Each of the brand new "tract" homes in suburban Lakewood Gardens was about 1,000 square feet, had three bedrooms, one bathroom, and a fireplace. There were seven models in the development, located within walking distance of a public elementary school and the first-ever outdoor shopping mall, Lakewood Center. The homes, bounded by dairies, alfalfa, and bean fields, cost between $10,400 and $10,600.

In 1953, my parents brought me home from my birth at Corona Naval Hospital, and, along with my three older siblings, we settled into life in this brand new, all-white community on the southern edge of Los Angeles County. My preschool, and later, my Girl Scout meetings convened at the Lakewood Gardens Civic Association Clubhouse. I learned how to make the Girl Scout Sign by raising the three middle fingers of my right hand as I recited the Girl Scout Promise:

> On my honor, I will try:
> To serve God and my country,
> To help people at all times,
> And to obey the Girl Scout Law.

Ever notice the difference between the Boy Scout's and Girl Scout's promise? The girls are going to "try."

I also learned the Girl Scout Law:

> I will do my best to be honest and fair,
> friendly and helpful, considerate and
> caring, courageous and strong, and
> responsible for what I say and do, and
> to respect myself and others, respect

authority, use resources wisely, make the
world a better place, and
be a sister to every Girl Scout.

All the little girls in my troop were white, and I assumed them as my referenced "sisters." I still have my dark green sash with merit badges fore and aft, as well as my Handbooks, evidencing years of encouragement to explore new interests and goals.

Ours was a very musical household. A piano was the first piece of furniture my parents purchased and moved into our house. My father sang barbershop, and my mother was a classically trained pianist who played stride and ragtime. I thought every family stood around the piano and harmonized. I had the opportunity to take lessons in piano, tap dancing, baton twirling, ice skating, and pretty much anything that interested me. Like most working-class families, we shopped for clothes three times a year—once in the fall for school clothes, once in the spring for Easter, and once for summertime. When we came home from school, we kids immediately changed from our school clothes into our play clothes. We played Three Flies Up and Freeze Tag out in the street until the streetlights came on. And if we were playing inside at a friend's house, it was understood that when the man of the house came home, it was dinnertime and you had to go home. Our family was a member of an all-white church and attended Sunday school regularly, said grace before meals, and knelt to say our bedtime prayers.

My father instilled civic values and the observance of every special day of remembrance, not only in the hearts of his four offspring but into those of the kids on our block as well. In the summertime, my father would organize us as miniature color guards to post and retire the flag each day. We would gather in the morning at the garage in back of our house and "prepare the colors," which meant the assigned color bearer would carefully unfold the flag and affix it to the flagpole, being extremely careful not to let it touch the ground. "Color guard, advance," he would announce. We children would solemnly march single file down our driveway, make a snappy left turn, and assemble in front of the porch steps. "Color guard, post the colors," he'd continue. We would then ascend the three steps to the porch landing and post the flag in the standard. "Color guard, honor your colors." We would salute the flag, put our small hands over our sincere hearts, and repeat the Pledge of Allegiance.

To conclude this flag ceremony, we reversed our steps and marched back to the garage. "Color guards dismissed," and off we'd go for the adventures of the day. At dusk, we would once again assemble at the garage and proceed back to the porch. "Color guard, retire the colors." We would then take the flag from the standard, march it back to the garage, fold it into that very particular triangle, and sing *Taps* accompanied by my oldest brother on the bugle. "Color guard dismissed." This pageantry allowed me to bask in the glorious time and attention bestowed upon me by my father.

As I think back on these childhood memories, I'm reminded of who I am and where I come from. I feel pride when I see the flag, and goosebumps when I hear the national anthem. These two important symbols signify respect and loyalty towards my country. My patriotic parents even taught me the specific manner in how our flag should and should not be displayed (U.S. Flag Code: Chapter 10.176C). What could have been more American than life in Lakewood Gardens and the GI Bill?

I was shocked to learn, decades later, that these same VA mortgages and the economic opportunities of home-ownership were not awarded to black veterans. And that the National Association of Realtors had prohibited non-white Realtors from joining the organization. I only learned of this when, as a licensed Realtor, I attended a meeting of the National Association of Real Estate Brokers (NAREB). This trade organization is an equal opportunity civil rights advocacy organization for black real estate professionals, consumers, and communities in America founded in 1947. NAREB's vision is "Democracy in Housing!" I had no idea this group existed or that there was even a need for its mission.

In "Tomorrow's City Today," there was nothing so blatant as a "Whites Only" sign or a separate drinking fountain for "Colored" anywhere. None were needed. The codified lending practices of the VA and Federal Housing Administration institutionalized and perpetuated housing discrimination throughout the country. This is how it was. Federally-sanctioned denial of land ownership would keep people of color not only separate from whites but sepa-rate from the economic system in which the dramatic rise in the value of these homes, in the coming decades, cre-ated for property owners. Our family home in Lakewood, kept in the family for over seventy years, sold for a price that would have been unimaginable by my parents. We happily grew up in this house, and then benefited from the economic power of its astonishing equity gain. The denial of this same financial opportunity to black and brown families, based solely on their race, ties me as a direct benefactor to the legally codified past oppression of people of color.

Soon after settling into Lakewood Gardens, my father retired from a thirty-three-year Navy career, and became, United States Postal Service (USPS) Postmaster of the Lakewood Branch. A photo and story that ran in the *Long Beach Press Telegram* in December 1960 shows my father standing in front of the Lakewood Post Office beside a brightly decorated, full sized, Santa's mailbox. I remember watching as he dedicatedly painted this magical creation in our backyard. Once installed, neighborhood children excitedly dropped off their letters to Santa at the North Pole. And if they included a return address, they received a reply back from Santa himself. This was the sort of wonder and playfulness my father, himself a Pearl Harbor survivor, brought to my childhood.

The following summer, my father decided to take a trip to visit his aging father, Silas, the infamous fire and brimstone Baptist preacher. Plans were made and happily, my brother John and I were allowed to go along on a cross-country trip aboard the Santa Fe train to Burlington, Iowa. I took with me the hit sensation of that summer—a Barbie doll. The visit with my grandfather Silas included snapping green beans on the porch, using an outhouse, and bathing in a galvanized tub in the kitchen. I experienced the magic of fireflies for the first time. These were beloved memories to make with both my father and my brother John, six years my senior.

When we returned home, I started the school year as a third-grader with newly expanded horizons. Four months later, during our Christmas break, my father was rushed to the hospital with a pulmonary embolism. At about 6:00 a.m. the next morning, my mother and sister awakened me and walked me into the living room. I sat sleepily between the two of them on our blue and green floral Naugahyde couch. My mother, as gently as possible, broke the news to me, my father had died during the night. The words washed over me as I searched their faces for meaning. My first response was, "Was he shot?" At my young age, I understood shooting as one of the ways life ends. When she answered "No," I remember feeling relieved my father hadn't died that violent way. They then both watched as I stood up and, as if in a dream, walked to the rotary dial telephone over by the floor heater and called my friend two doors down to tell her the news. I didn't know up from down. I had said goodbye to my father the morning before as I skipped out to play, never dreaming he would be gone from me when I returned home.

The next time I saw my father was at White's Funeral Home. I reached into the open casket to touch his handsome face, and quickly pulled my hand back, recoiling at the coldness of his skin. I asked my mother if we couldn't just keep his body with us at home, so deep was my longing not to be separated from him. At the funeral, I sat next to my brother John and was silently permitted to cry as I watched massive tears rolling down his cheeks. This moment was perhaps the last time my family openly expressed its profound grief together. From then on, we individually processed his absence alone, each in our own way. For me, his death brought a numbing end to my childhood and produced a jumble of misperceptions about life—that it was unfair, that it owed me something, that this loss was somehow my fault.

The week following my father's death was Christmas. I had been asking for a puppy, and apparently my father wanted to make sure I got one. On Christmas morning, there was a note with my name on it that said "Follow the string." An elaborate trail led me through the house, out the front door, around a tree, across the street, and up to the neighbor's porch. When I knocked, they opened the front door and out bounded a gray puppy wagging its tail exuberantly, with a bright red bow around her neck. The addition of a puppy to help heal my wounded heart was a loving and hopeful idea, yet overwhelming at the same time. A few weeks later, we were out playing on the back porch and I tried to get her to come through a wrought iron railing. She wasn't coming and I became frustrated, then angry, and pulled her through, hard. She yelped and cried, and kept crying. I was terrified, guilty, and ashamed. A trip to the vet showed a dislocated hip. She was put in a cast and, thankfully, made a full recovery. But within the layers of trauma, there was no place to understand or process the emotions churning within me and my family.

My mother fought hard with the VA to establish that my father's death was service-connected and succeeded in having his GI benefits awarded to the family. Again, I had no idea these resources were available to us because of our whiteness. Coming from a long line of the Society of Friends on one side, and Disciples of Christ on the other, my mother had earned a bachelor's degree in Social Work from California Christian College, which later became Chapman College. Now as a single mother, it was necessary for her to work full-time to support the family.

Through the help of one of our neighbors, also a social worker, my mother got a job at Long Beach Children's

Clinic, Serving Children & Their Families. Many times after school, I kept myself occupied at the clinic while my mother finished work. The clinic's administrator's name, was coincidentally, Kay Baker, a big, strong, white woman with a shock of gray hair. Late one afternoon, I watched as my mother turned in her laboriously handwritten case notes. Kay took one look at the reports and tore them in half, "These are worthless. They have no date on them," she said. From that day forward, my mother and I dated everything, even our grocery lists! In addition to Kay's lifelong commitment to serving the community, she devotedly raised, trained, and showed Italian Greyhounds. Kay convinced us a more suitable home was needed for my puppy, now growing into a large, energetic, Weimaraner. She found her a forever home and then gifted me with an Italian Greyhound. Over the next ten years, Kay included me in her life as her aide-de-camp. We built glass bottle walls, poured concrete patios, cleared brush, and mended fencing. Her standard phrase to me was "You can do it." In this, and in a myriad of other ways, Kay was part of the village that raised me, a strong female role model for my new normal.

I often went along with my mother delivering items such as baby formula to low-income families living in nearby Carmelitos Housing Project. Developers created housing projects such as Avalon Gardens, Estrada Courts, and Hacienda Village in South Los Angeles. Numerous street gangs are named for the projects from which they emerged. A look at the map seems to show how the Los Angeles freeways created isolation of racial communities, reinforcing lines of segregation, and further contributing to homogeneous communities.

It was on these visits to Carmelitos with my mother, I saw people of color for the first time. The residents of the projects seemed so different from me, maybe even a different species. They scared me. This perception was, in part, fueled by the firm tone in my mother's instructions to "keep the car doors locked." I saw poverty for the first time and wondered why these individuals were living in such an ugly place. I was oblivious to the easy mobility I had that these people of color did not. As a nine-year-old, I came to see my mother as a hero, a white savior to these victims. This ethic to "do good" and to serve was deeply instilled in all the Baker kids and with it the unspoken, embedded feeling of superiority over those poor unfortunates, my mother's "care packages." I wondered why these people didn't get themselves up and out of this dismal, discouraging place. Did they somehow like it, prefer it there? Or, perhaps it was because, as has often mistakenly been assumed by those of higher station, poverty is synonymous with stupidity.

There was one particular family living in Carmelitos, with whom my mother bonded. My mother was always saving our special castoffs for them. Several times a year, our two families would share home-cooked holiday foods and exchange small gifts at our home. My mother's relationship with the black mother seemed careful, as if she didn't quite know how to be with the other woman, but a genuine affection and respect for her was apparent. The black mother, on the other hand, seemed to know quite well how to relate to a white woman effectively. The members of this family were the only individuals of color I knew. While a pejorative word about another race was not allowed within our home, the programming of "us" and "them" was abundantly clear. Even as a young child, I'm ashamed to say I felt I must be somehow smarter and above these people of color who seemed to be so stuck in their situation. In the coming days, just a few months before the legendary March on Washington in 1963, a Freedom Protest was held at Wrigley Field in Los Angeles. I was only ten years old. I didn't know anyone who attended, and for me it was a non-event.

✳ ✳ ✳

THERE WAS ALWAYS SHEET music on the piano in our living room, awaiting my mother to sit down and play. I well remember her playing the songs from the 1940s hit musical *South Pacific* written by Oscar Hammerstein and Richard Rodgers. Within the score is the song "You've Got to be Carefully Taught" (1949). Quite controversial in its day, the lyrics suggest discrimination is not inherent, that no child is born to naturally fear and hate.

While it was modeled by my mother and my Sunday school teacher that hating other people was wrong, I had no regular participation in the lives of different races or ethnicities. Yes, the Golden Rule said to "love your neighbor," but all my neighbors were white. I knew of no one involved in the civil rights movement. Thanks to my older siblings, I was familiar with the folk music of the early 1960s such as Peter Seeger, Peter Paul & Mary, and Joe and Eddie. Bob Dylan's protest songs had shed light on the terrible violence and injustices taking place in the Jim Crow South. Joan Baez had performed songs such as "We Shall Overcome" and "Oh Freedom." But in my part of America, I was unaware of any one who was listening. Back in Lakewood Gardens, nothing beyond the more catchy folk tunes penetrated our white cocoon. This milieu was the culture of my childhood, my upbringing.

At the Freedom Protest at Wrigley Field, Martin Luther King Jr. had told the audience, "We want to be free whether we're in Birmingham or in Los Angeles." The Civil Rights Act did pass the following year, but California passed its own Proposition 14, giving all property owners the right to refuse to sell, rent, or lease their property based solely on race. Although ruled unconstitutional, this right remained in effect for another ten years. As a white child growing up in segregated Los Angeles, I had no concept of how white advantages were at work to create black disadvantages.

I was attending the fourth grade of all-white Captain Raymond Collins Elementary School, located just a few blocks from home. Like most kids in the Los Angeles Unified School District, I was taught the history of my state that year through the romanticized story of how Father Junípero Serra colonized Alta California through the Spanish mission system. There was a requisite art project associated with this history lesson in which we created a miniature version of one of the twenty-one missions—basically a slave plantation. There was no mention of California's very own Trail of Tears—The Owen's Valley Indian War—in which native California's tribes, such as the Paiute, Shoshone, and Kawaiisu, were removed by either genocide or marched to the Sebastian Indian Reservation near Fort Tejon. This narrative, the normalizing of violence against "others," was presented to us without question, and simply as historical facts.

On television, local Los Angeles kid shows like *Sheriff John*, *Engineer Bill*, and the local affiliate of *Romper Room*, featured only white characters and commercials.

At the nearby May Company and Butler Brother's stores, all the mannequins were white. We lived in what was called a "good" neighborhood, anchored to the monocultural experiences provided therein. Whiteness was the standard, the norm, the baseline. We had glass bottles of milk delivered to our doors, visits from the Helms Bakery truck, and door-to-door salespeople purveying all manner of goods to meet our domestic needs. A particular group of good-humored neighbors routinely planned elaborate practical jokes on each other involving the imaginary "ooo-ack" bird. On my mothers' fiftieth birthday, a candlelight choir of about thirty neighbors stood on our front lawn and sang her a Happy Birthday. The close-knit homogeneous community with all its civic values created a powerful sense of "we," a sort of collective soul of "our" community. Something akin to this landscape is familiar to most every white child who grew up in a segregated, blue-collar suburb in the 1950s and 1960s, replicated all across America.

I have a colorized portrait of me in full cowgirl regalia atop a Shetland pony taken in our driveway. I had just walked home from kindergarten, wearing my favorite plaid dress and black patent leather shoes. I remember begging my mother to please let the photographer and pony stop, and the joy when she did so. Like many little girls, I was horse crazy. My best friend lived one block over and she also had a horse bedspread, horse rug, and horse lamp. Like me, she had lost a parent several years previously. My friend and I, both "half-orphans," shared a sense of aloneness, of not quite belonging in the world. When someone later in life enlightened me to the fact that most superheroes are orphans, I could understand that drive, that need, to get out there and right the grievous wrongs of injustice. That drive is also a desire to know connection, solidarity, and standing together. When my friend and I were in the sixth grade, our two families bought us one horse to share, a pinto mare named Tammy. We boarded Tammy at Juan De Cordova stables in Long Beach, where we two earnest, little cowgirls spent every free moment riding the unpaved, unfenced San Gabriel River bed from dawn till dusk. Loving and caring for Tammy gave us both the opportunity to heal. Again, I was unaware that my family having resources significant enough to make my childhood dream come true was by virtue of our race.

But there was a sharp contrast to this idyll, a simmering burn which exploded in 1965. In February, there was something on the news about the assassination of a violent black man by the name of Malcolm X, who I think I overheard hated white people. It's a hazy memory, but there seemed to be a feeling that he had somehow gotten what he deserved for one reason or another. That August, the nearby Watts Riots erupted after a contentious arrest situation involving the South Central police. Thousands of National Guardsmen descended on Southern California to restore order as rioter's looted stores, torched buildings, and fired at police officers and firefighters. "Just look at those people, burning down their community," one of my oldest siblings had said. When I asked why these riots were happening, no one in my sphere had an answer to what seemed to be this pointless destruction, and no understanding of its cause and effect. But it didn't really matter because whatever was going on in Compton wasn't our problem. Except when it was getting a little too close to home.

Again, I had the pervasive sense of "us" versus "them," now fueled with an increasing fear of the violence and crime associated with people of color. In segregated Southern California, if there were conversations about or participation in the civil rights movement, it didn't include me. If my family was involved, I was unaware of it. Perhaps there was an element of simply protecting me from the ugliness of the world. As an adult, I did see footage of white activists marching in Selma for Civil Rights, and this was the only example I had of white individuals getting personally involved in racial justice. But this was happening far away in Selma, Alabama where they indeed had race problems. The March on Washington for Jobs and Freedom happened that August when Martin Luther King Jr. delivered his "I Have a Dream" speech. Joan Baez sang "When the Ship Comes In" with Bob Dylan, and Dylan performed, "Only a Pawn in Their Game," concerning the assassination of black civil rights activist Medgar Evers. I know all this only by looking back. At the time, as a twelve-year-old white girl living in "Tomorrow's City Today," these were simply stories in the news about other people in other places. Where I lived, there weren't any race problems, and until recently, I never wondered why.

Two years later, during the "Long Hot Summer of 1967," there were 159 race riots in cities across the United States. I was fourteen. President Johnson ordered an investigation as to why these riots occurred. Seven months later, the Report of the National Advisory Commission on Civil Disorders was released, and two million Americans bought copies. While I was too young and unaffected to read it, the report found the riots resulted from black frustration at the lack of economic opportunity and made numerous recommendations on how to address this disparity.

At the time, Martin Luther King Jr. called the report "a physician's warning of approaching death, with a prescription for life." The report said, "The press has too long basked in a white world looking out of it, if at all, with white men's eyes and white perspective." An essential line from the report stated: "Our nation is moving toward two societies, one black, one white—separate and unequal." But its recommendations were at the time largely ignored. Any attempts by my white family to understand the violent unrest and protest within the black community were akin to trying to understand a game just by watching its players (Irving 2014).

I lived in racially segregated Lakewood Gardens throughout my elementary school years, and my older siblings attended Alondra Junior High and Paramount High School located northeast of Lakewood. The City of Paramount, a predominantly Hispanic community also known as "Little Sinaloa," was about three miles from our house. The City of Compton, a mostly black community, was about five miles away, bordering Watts. I started taking figure skating lessons at Paramount's Iceland Skating Rink, home of the Zamboni ice resurfacing machine. My brothers cruised Bellflower Boulevard on the weekends in their Chevy Impalas, hanging out with guys and their lowriders. The Jolly Roger yearbook from Paramount High School in the late 1960s shows the cultural mix of whites and Hispanics.

By the time I started seventh grade at Alondra Jr. High, the neighborhood boys I grew up were wearing white T-shirts, Pendleton's, and baggy khaki's. My girlfriends and I practiced teasing our hair high and applying thick makeup. We rode loud, homemade mini-cycles up and down our street. We were growing up and testing our boundaries. A few of my closest friends began experimenting with drugs, dangerous drugs. Our world was rocked when a beloved classmate, living four doors down, died from an accidental heroin overdose in the family garage.

My three older siblings had by now graduated from Paramount High School and my mother decided we were going to leave Lakewood Gardens. Again, I took for granted the options and resources available to us that were not available to people of color and lower economic status in the neighboring communities. Whatever multicultural experiences I had thus far were about to end. My mother refinanced our steadily appreciating house for a small down payment on a modest townhouse, and she and I moved from our increasingly "rough" neighborhood in South Los Angeles County to homogeneous white Orange County and into the land of promise.■

My parent's engagement in Laguna Mountains, CA, ca. 1939.
Carolyn L. Baker Family Archives.

My baby shower at Lakewood Gardens Clubhouse in 1953. *Carolyn L. Baker Family Archives.*

The Silas Baker family reunion in our backyard, in Lakewood Gardens, ca. 1955. *Carolyn L. Baker Family Archives.*

My father, Lt. Cmdr. Earl Ross Baker (r) and brother Stan (l), in Long Beach, CA, ca. 1950. *Carolyn L. Baker Family Archives.*

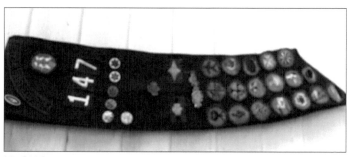

My Girl Scout sash and merit badges. *Carolyn. L. Baker Family Archives.*

Me posing for the ubiquitous Shetland pony picture, taken in our driveway in Lakewood, ca. 1957. *Carolyn. L. Baker Family Archives.*

A Baker family photo in front of the piano, with me in my father's arms in Lakewood Gardens, 1953. *Carolyn. L. Baker Family Archives.*

Lakew

The

"LA

OL. 9 — NO. 101   TOrrey 7-1763

SANTA'S MAIL BOX

SPECIAL DELIVERY TO NORTH POLE— Lakewood Postmaster Earl R. Baker, here shows off "Santa's Mailbox", erected early this week on the steps of the local postoffice. Local youngsters, using this special delivery box, may be sure that letters to the good saint will reach the North Pole before Christmas. Mailbox and Christmas decorations that surround the postal facility were erected last Sunday by employees working on their own time.

Enterprise Photo

My father, Postmaster Earl Baker at Santa's Mailbox, USPS Lakewood Branch, 1960. *Carolyn. L. Baker Family Archives.*

The Baker family in 1963, two years after my father passed away, when the neighbors of Lakewood Gardens threw a surprise 50th birthday party for my mother (c). I am standing next to my mother. *Carolyn. L. Baker Family Archives.*

CHAPTER 2

Social Consciousness

"And each time I feel like this inside, there's one thing
I wanna know: What's so funny 'bout peace love &
understanding?" —**Nick Lowe, 1973**

L OW-INCOME PEOPLE OF COLOR in Los Angeles County
were nonexistent in our new neighborhood in Orange
County. My nearly all-white, brand spanking new Los
Alamitos High School, was an avant-garde social experiment right in the middle of the Anaheim Unified School
District. Many of the teachers were not much older than
the students, and during its first two years, the school had
a flexible scheduling program. Each morning we'd meet
in our scheduling groups assigned alphabetically by our
last names, and complete a hand-written daily schedule
in 15-minute modules. We could choose from regularly
scheduled classes, or write in "sitting on the grass." This
setting of freedom and support for our creativity and
imagination was a gift awarded to a particular, fortunate
few living within the right school district.

There was certainly a different feeling between Los
Angeles and Orange counties, but I couldn't quite identify
what it was at the time. I missed my old neighborhood
friends and dreamed about my first crush, a boy from a
neighborhood just outside the boundaries of Lakewood

Gardens. I missed the Los Angeles County cultures from which we had fled. I met two girls whose families had also recently relocated from Los Angeles County, and we teamed up to bolster each other's quest to redefine ourselves in this new culture. I found my tribe in the Vocal Music Department, a place where the musician in me would be nurtured and further developed. Also, having had the good fortune of childhood dance classes, I tried out for the pom-pom line, the Song Girls, and made it. The bright path of opportunity was mine to take, and I did. These activities set my course firmly on the extracurricular, social side of life at Los Alamitos High School, where my peers were all white and of the same socioeconomic class as me. I recall no real friendships with other nationalities, races, or ethnicities.

My family had military privileges at nearby Los Alamitos Air Force Base, where we shopped at the commissary, went bowling, and went to the movie theater. I got an officer's sticker due to my father's rank in the Navy on my red Corvair Monza. Each time I approached the gates at the entrance to the base, the servicemen standing at their posts saluted me. This honor, shown to me as a sixteen-year-old girl, created deeply conflicting feelings—pride in my father whom I deeply missed, a budding opposition to the military and the Vietnam War, and embarrassment for honor shown that was not rightfully mine. The freedom of having a car allowed me to land my first of many waitressing jobs at a local steakhouse, thanks to a reference from a family friend.

Statewide, the Haight-Ashbury district in San Francisco just had the "Summer of Love," and Southern California had the Elysian Park Love In. Held on Easter Sunday, the Love-In coincided with the Spring Equinox, and posters proclaimed it as "an offering to the City of Los Angeles." In announcing the event, Art Kunkin's *Los Angeles Free Press* wrote, "The ceremony will be carefully prepared in accordance with the movements of the sun and the metaphysical doctrines of the spring equinox. As the morning turns to afternoon, the park grounds will become alive with thousands of beautiful people exchanging simple gifts (apples, oranges, incense, etc.), listening to music, moving around ceremonial tents, breathing deeply, digging life, and loving each other."[1] A friend who attended described the day this way, "It was so beautiful, all ages and all races joining together to proclaim the Brotherhood of Man. Here in Southern California, it seemed to me things were different from the troubles elsewhere, particularly the blatant discrimination in the South. Here I thought there was inclusion and equality."

✳ ✳ ✳

EVEN FROM WITHIN the sheltered world of Orange County, I began to see things in alternative ways—a phenomenon happening with young people across the nation. The Vietnam War was escalating and with it a growing dissent concerning American institutions. There were discussions at school about government corruption, the evils of capitalism and a materialistic culture, and the military-industrial complex. Yet, I never questioned why there weren't any black students living in my neighborhood, or in my Los Alamitos High School Class of 1971, which appeared to be done by deliberate social engineering. The new draft lottery discriminated against the low-educated and low-income

---

1. Quote used with permission, courtesy of the Los Angeles Free Press, http://LosAngelesFreePress.com, Steven M. Finger, Publisher.

class and, while I was beginning to recognize the discrimination and racial injustice at hand, I wasn't as motivated to protest the draft on those grounds. I was opposed to it based on moral, ethical, and religious beliefs—as a conscientious objector, as my Quaker forebears had been.

"To say we are mired in stalemate seems the only realistic, if unsatisfactory, conclusion."[2] CBS newsman Walter Cronkite had said at the closing of a particularly horrifying program showing the real faces of war. *The Smothers Brothers Show* and *Laugh-In* were bringing the other side of the party line, as is part of the job of the comedians. Radical groups such as The Diggers in San Francisco were committed to overt political opposition to the war. There was a movement in which young, middle class, white youth could actively participate—the Peace Movement in opposition to the Vietnam War. Martin Luther King Jr. had said the Vietnam War was devastating the hopes of the poor at home. If people of poverty were the largest demographic of those dying on the front lines, then this was, tangentially, one way I "joined" the civil rights movement.

In the spring of 1968, Dr. King delivered his final sermon, "Remaining Awake Through a Great Revolution." He urged support for The Poor People's Campaign, and the need to acknowledge the deep roots of racism in America and the effects of the tragedies of racial injustice. Dr. King was assassinated five days later in Memphis, and riots broke out in over 100 American cities. My disconnect regarding other races was so significant, I have no recollection of even watching the story of his murder on the news. So shielded was I, I have no memory of ever discussing it. It was to

---

2.   Walter Cronkite, "We Are Mired in Stalemate." Commentary on CBS News Special Report, February 27, 1968.

me inconsequential. Then, the assassination of Robert F. Kennedy at the Ambassador Hotel in Los Angeles followed several months later. Both of these murders took a back seat to the issues concerning me as a teenage girl—my hair, my clothes, and trying to fit in. Although my disconnect at this age may have been more developmental than political, these assassinations barely registered with me.

Over Christmas break that same year, our Los Alamitos High School choir director took his life. Returning to campus, choir members were shuttled immediately into rehearsals with a substitute music teacher to prepare a song for the memorial service. I remember the faces of the devastated choir students as they responded to this shock. One of the downsides of white privilege is a sense of invulnerability, this fantasy of safety and security. Perhaps my acquaintance with the impermanence of life through the early loss of my father had made me a bit more ready to deal with a loss of this sort as part of life. When the relative of a classmate attempted suicide later that year, our teacher called me out of class to accompany them home. In much the same way we teach what we need to learn, holding the hands of friends and loved ones at the end of their lives would continue into my adulthood.

There was an English course at Los Alamitos High School entitled "Rock Poetry." The course was post-Woodstock, and we discussed lyrics protesting the Vietnam War and songs by singer/songwriters living in Los Angeles' Laurel Canyon. Overt political activism was mixing with a general alienation from the status quo. This was for me less of a political drive and more of a politics of no politics. A dear friend, a "lifer" in the Los Angeles music scene, had this to say about the cultural evolution reflected in the music, "Pre-Beatles, folk music was largely about the human condition, social justice, and civil rights. Folk music was the window into the full story of life in America. After those days, protest music began to be almost laughable, thought of as soft and cute. But it wasn't."

The hippie movement was separating us white middle-class youth from mainstream culture through our appearance and lifestyle, even in cookie-cutter Orange County. Franco Zeffirelli's *Romeo and Juliet* was out in the theaters, and I became enamored of the costumes and music. I sewed beautiful period dresses and joined a recorder consort group which performed at local Renaissance Faire's, festivals, and the first Earth Day. Our new choir director, Fred Frank, was a professional entertainer who considerably elevated our musicianship and took us out into the community-at-large to perform. At the same time, as Benvolio said in *Romeo and Juliet,* "For now these hot days is the mad blood stirring." Concurrent with the soft protest of the hippies, there was an increasing militancy within the Black Power movement emphasizing racial pride, black political and cultural institutions, and promoting black interests and values. In Rock Poetry class, we talked about the Soledad Brothers, Eldridge Cleaver, and Angela Davis. Particularly, we talked about an interview with Angela Davis while she was in prison in California, in which she was asked by Canadian author and filmmaker Barry Callaghan how she felt about the "violence" of the Black Power movement:

> "When I was living in Los Angeles, I was constantly stopped. The police didn't know who I was, but I was a Black woman, and I had a natural, and I suppose they thought that I might be a 'militant.'

You live under that situation constantly, and then you ask me whether I approve of violence. I mean, that just doesn't make any sense at all. Whether I approve of guns? I grew up in Birmingham, Alabama. Some very good friends of mine were killed by bombs that were planted by racists. From the time I was very small, I remember the sounds of bombs exploding across the street, our house shaking. I remember my father having to have guns at his disposal at all times because of the fact that at any moment, we might expect to be attacked" (Callaghan 1971).

Her words were a revelation to me. For the first time, I began glimpsing the cause and effect relationship between decades of overt racist actions, everyday violence of poverty, and lack of opportunity and the black militancy of the day from which I had been sheltered up to this point. Taken even further, her words reflected the cumulative effect of centuries of Western colonialism and oppression. Callaghan was fired from the Canadian network he worked for shortly after the Davis interview was broadcast.

This English class and its inspiring teacher were the beginnings of my awakening into things other than my own lived experience. Tommie Smith, Peter Norman, and John Carlos demonstrated for human rights in a political protest on the Olympic podium in Mexico City. My family was offended at the irreverence of the raised fists at this most sacred gathering where all races, cultures, and countries came together to build a peaceful and better world without discrimination of any kind. These negative actions weren't in the Olympic spirit! The reality of this very public protest of racial injustice, set amid the backdrop of the American flag, forced the admonition of troubles in our homeland. It was both frightening and awakening to me.

While the general hippie credo was peace and non-violence, the yippies demonstrated and got arrested. When asked to differentiate between the hippies and the yippies, Abby Hoffman said, "a Yippie is a Hippie who has been beaten by police." The differing approach of the Black Power movement and the yippies seemed to be to fight fire with fire, while the response of the hippies was to use water to put out the fire. "Turn on, tune in, and drop out" was the mantra of the day, as per Timothy Leary, and a common distrust of "the man." *Hair: The American Tribal Love-Rock Musical* had come to town, bolstering the public to demand change — to exercise their rights to protest, to vote for a better tomorrow. Or, as Langston Hughes put it, an America that never has been yet.

I read *The Book: On the Taboo Against Knowing Who You Are* (1966), *The Crack in the Cosmic Egg* (1971), and *Be Here Now* (1971). I explored Vedanta philosophy and spiritual paths to experiencing love and consciousness. It was a wake-up experience cultivating awareness and mindfulness. In this "Age of Aquarius" in 1968, I was listening to The Beatles' *White Album* and the Rolling Stones' *Beggar's Banquet,* and watched the movies *2001: A Space Odyssey* (1968) and *Planet of the Apes* (1968). My teachers, classmates, and I participated in the very first nationwide Earth Day, planting trees on campus under which Los Alamitos High School students sit today. Several months later, two oil tankers, the Arizona Standard and the Oregon Standard, collided spilling 800,000 gallons of crude oil into the San Francisco Bay. Thousands of volunteers cleaned up beaches and rescued oil-soaked birds. One of these environmental activists was a young black man named John Francis who decided to do his part by not using a car for transportation. Francis started walking and found himself arguing with folks in his neighborhood about whether or not one person could make a real difference by not using a car. He decided to completely stop talking for one day. That one day turned into walking in silence for seventeen years. In his inspiring presentations, and books, Dr. John Francis, also known as Planetwalker, explains that, while the environment is about human-made ugliness, pollution, and endangered species, it is really much more than that. It is about human rights, and civil rights, and economic equity. It involves how we treat each other when we meet each other." [3]

My eyes were beginning to open, an awakening that was more than a trend. By the middle of my senior year, I had dropped out of the Song Girls, stopped straightening my naturally wavy hair, and became a vegetarian. There had even been the burning of American flags on the Los Alamitos High School campus. It was happening all over the nation. The English teacher who had been an inspiration to my opening mind and heart, wrote in my Cottonwood yearbook, "So much to say and yet what can I say? We have learned much from each other. Your openness has helped me to be more open. If we can keep open and give of ourselves, we will see the lives of others take shape. I'm glad we have come to know each other. Love and Life Together. GIVE!"[4]

---

3. John Francis "We Must Stop Exploiting the Planet," TEDx Oil Spill, August 15, 2011. https://www.youtube.com/watch?v=Gaq7SthTTHg.

4. Lavelle Foos, *The Cottonwood Yearbook*, Alamitos High School. 1971.

In the last month of my senior year at Los Alamitos High School, I met a handsome surfer, the first-generation American son of hardworking immigrant parents. His father had immigrated from Italy and his mother from Mexico. The family was following the American dream of property ownership in the form of owning and operating motels. Three generations of the family lived on the property and ate and worked together. I fell deeply in love with him, his family, and the beautiful Latin cultures. The family referred to me as Carolina, a name I still cherish and, in some circles, go by today. Amid a blissed-out year of bell bottoms, long hair, and back-to-the-land living, we all scrubbed toilets and made beds.

If Abraham Maslow's hierarchy of needs holds, we were a tidal wave of young people, mostly middle-class, educated whites from suburban backgrounds, with our basic survival and coping needs met. My need for food, shelter, safety, connection, and esteem were all squared away, thanks to the increasing Post-war affluence of the white community. I was not the target of discrimination or oppression faced by other racial and economic groups. Rather, I was motivated and enabled to address the higher-order needs of Self-Actualization and Transcendence—finding my place in society, my identity, and expanding my spiritual consciousness. And for many of the hippies "doing their own thing," a cynicism, even a complacency, was creeping in. A musician friend summed it up when she recalled, "One night I walked into The Troubadour near the Sunset Strip and, just to try something, announced 'Hey, I just heard the Vietnam War is over' and no one even really reacted." ■

Here I am, a Song Girl at Los Alamitos High School, striking a typical pose, 1971. *Carolyn L. Baker Family Archives.*

Me on a winter surfing adventure, Ensenada, Mexico, 1972.
Carolyn L. Baker Family Archives.

CHAPTER 3

SOCIAL SERVICE

"The opposite of love is not hate, it's indifference."
—Elie Wiesel, Nobel writer and Auschwitz survivor

IN 1972, MY MAN AND I connected with a joyous counter-cultural group, the Jesus People. The Jesus movement was based on evangelical Christianity and existed out-side of traditional mainstream churches. We west coast followers sought to return to the original life of the early Christians, with simple lifestyles and communal living. Jesus music and live concerts were a dynamic draw for us rock 'n roll loving young people. We attended intensive bible studies, highlighting the especially meaningful pas-sages. A contemporary image of Jesus with the heading "The Jesus Revolution" had made the cover of *Time Magazine* (June 21, 1971).

On March 4, 1973, my surfer-turned-"brother" and I married. I was nineteen. I wore a white muslin peasant dress that I made myself and a floral wreath in my waist-length hair. The reception was held at the Lakewood Gardens Civic Association Clubhouse. My new Italian father-in-law, also a Navy man, affectionately referred to me as "Little Daughter," a tribute to my father. My own daughter was born the following year, by natural childbirth. My husband and I decided to open our home to communal living for the church group we had joined. Our hearts were in the right place, and we had a longing to dedicate ourselves to a higher purpose and ideal. I also believe I genuinely needed and wanted to connect, to be part of a community.

Soon we were happily expecting our second child. We had between four to six college students, "brothers," living with us and we all were attending California State University, Long Beach (CSULB). As is often true with group identities, there was a constant and robust feeling of our "rightness," and the "wrongness" of outsiders, the binary "us" versus "them." At the time, I saw this living arrangement as both appropriate and righteous. One afternoon I pulled into the CSULB parking lot late for my English Literature class. There were no parking spots to be found, save the blue designated handicapped spaces. Justifying to myself that I was sort of handicapped, being six months pregnant and all, I parked in the blue space and headed across campus to class. Never mind I didn't have a special parking permit. When I returned to my car there was, as expected, a ticket on the windshield. We didn't have the discretionary income to pay for a parking ticket, so I decided to write a letter explaining myself. The president of the Disabled Students Union took the time to write me back, asking if I cared to attend their weekly meeting and express, in person, my inconvenience and entitlement. Embarrassed at being called out, I paid the ticket.

My family and close friends became growingly concerned as my behavior began to change. As a young family, we stopped celebrating traditional "pagan" holidays such as Christmas and Easter. I penned a Letter to the Editor publicly condemning homosexuality, that was printed in the *Long Beach Press Telegram*, in which I made strong biblical references to "one man, one woman." I admit this with apologies.

When our second child was born, the pressures of maintaining the communal household as well as conforming to the top-down patriarchy made me wonder about my sanity. But it was hard to argue with what seemed at the time to be God. When a "brother" committed a crime in my home, I took the issue to my husband, who took it to the elders who said they would handle it. There was no police report made or charges brought.

What had been abundantly clear to most everyone around us was that this lifestyle was becoming unsustainable. Using the respiratory health of our young son as a valid excuse, we left the church in Southern California and relocated to Arizona in the summer of 1978 for a fresh start. My young family had lived in five places in as many years.

✳ ✳ ✳

My social worker mother had instilled in me that "A college degree is something they can never take away from you," and I continually took at least one course every semester. I finally tied together enough credits, from five colleges and two states, to earn a teaching degree from Arizona State University, ten years after graduating from high school. At my graduation ceremony, I placed masking tape on the top of my mortarboard, spelling out the word M-O-M. My kids informed me that, from where they sat in the stadium, it read W-O-W, and that about summed it up. During those years, domestic violence escalated, and my husband and I, two people with a lot of personal baggage, increasingly triggered each other into a toxic and abusive marital relationship. A third save-the-marriage pregnancy had ended in a lonely and disheartening miscarriage. We were in the throes of yet another move, and, as a graduation present, my mother had come out to watch the kids so we could take a short vacation alone. We fought nearly the entire time.

I completed my student teaching assignment and landed a job as an adjunct professor teaching physical education and dance classes for Rio Salado Community College. The classes were well received and growing in popularity. With one last and ultimate marital betrayal, the decision I had previously been unable to make for my wellness, I now felt able to make for the sake of my children. Having the college degree gave me the confidence that I'd be able to somehow look out for us on my own.

Although it was excruciatingly painful to say goodbye to the cherished dream of an intact family, I moved my children and myself into a double-wide modular home in a small rural town and filed for divorce to end my nine-year marriage. A brutal custody battle ensued, further dismantling both me and my resources. After months of individual and group interviews, the fate of our family was determined by psychologists, attorneys, and a judge. I remember opening the letter and reading the court's decision as I stood alone in my kitchen while the kids were at school. The pages seemed to catch fire, as though my life was going up in flames. The court had granted custody to the children's father and ordered them to live with him and his new family, and for me to pay child support.

I was devastated. I felt I had failed at the most important role in my life—that of wife and mother. This shocking blow to my self-image and self-worth sent me into therapy and 12-step recovery programs. I took a sad, little temporary apartment nearby the children and their new family that matched my broken heart and spirit. One day I went to my mailbox and waiting there was a letter from a friend. I opened the envelope with a familiar sense of dread. What I found inside forever impacted my life. When I unfolded the letter, tucked inside was a check for $300. The letter explained the money was to help with my moving expenses at this difficult time, and that the money was a gift, not meant to be repaid. My friend had also known difficult times and understood the profound impact a simple act of kindness could have when life is hard.

From that moment on, I've always tried to remember just how far a little compassion and mercy can go. As Willy Wonka said, "So shines a good deed in a weary world."[1] It was not long before a new credentialing requirement came down, stating all community college instructors must have a graduate degree. During these seemingly dark days came the perfect opportunity for me to pull myself together, try a little harder, reach a bit further, and attack this new goal. I enrolled in extension courses through Northern Arizona University. And as things go, the children's living situation soon became untenable, the custody arrangement reversed, and they moved back home with me. My mother, now retired, graciously moved out of Los Angeles to be of help to me, keenly understanding the challenges of a single working mother.

These were years of working several jobs at a time, getting inadequate rest, being bone tired, as well as experiencing singularly glorious moments in the beauty of Arizona. Being both a mother and father to my children

1. *Willa Wonka and The Chocolate Factory*, directed by Mel Stuart (1971; Burbank, CA: Warner Bros). Reference to Portia in Shakespeare's *Merchant of Venice*.

when at times it was not humanly possible, I learned to live with perpetual fear, guilt, and anger when far too many bases were left uncovered. I remember one afternoon while driving the kid's home from school, I got so angry with their loud bickering in the back seat, I pulled over, made them get out of the car and walk the rest of the way home. I know I was not a model parent during those years, but I did the best I could at the time.

It took a while, again one course at a time, but seven years after earning the bachelor's degree, I completed a master's degree in Educational Psychology from Northern Arizona University in the winter of 1988. With these exciting new alphabets behind my name, I decided to see what, beyond teaching, might be out there for me.

There was an ad in the local newspaper for an Executive Director of a nonprofit hospital healthcare foundation. I looked up the word foundation to see what it meant. I must have presented appropriately, and got the job. Over the years, the stability of a good job, in this small rural town, allowed me to provide for myself and my family and to see them into high school.

One night while cooking dinner, I overheard from the television in the living room a news story about a black motorist, Rodney King, who was pulled over for speeding on a Los Angeles freeway. I stopped what I was doing and walked closer to the television in time to see the videotape of four white California Highway Patrol officers beating and kicking King dozens of times, including after he was on the ground. The images were horrifying. But out of necessity, my attention went right back to getting the kids fed, making sure their homework was done, preparing for the next work/school day, etc. – all the necessary tasks of a single mother working full time. But the images remained in my head.

A year later in 1992, the four officers were acquitted of felony assault. Los Angeles Mayor Tom Bradley had angrily said, "The jury's verdict will never blind the world to what we saw on the videotape."[2] Some called it officially sanctioned brutality and racism. As riots reflecting the frustration at the criminal justice system exploded in South Los Angeles, there was burning and looting of stores and attacks on non-black observers. Again the question was, this time posed to me by my own adolescent children, "Why are those people burning down their own neighborhood?" The National Guard was again sent in and in the end the Los Angeles Riots left more than fifty people dead, with damages exceeding hundreds of millions of dollars. Rodney King appeared on television and made the emotional plea for peace with his now-famous words, "Can't we all just get along?" It seemed there were two separate worlds.

My daughter expressed a desire to become a Catholic along with her high school friends. Her catechism teacher was a kind and gentle single man. We became friends and grew close. When he surprised me with a proposal of marriage, I asked him if I could think about it. Although it had been years since the divorce, I wasn't sure marriage was for me. Still, somehow I was a believer in the idea, and the security of a supportive partner was a welcome thought. I took the required Rite of Christian Initiation of Adults classes and became a Catholic. We married shortly

2. Richard A. Serrano and Tracy Wilkinson, "All 4 in King beating acquitted," Los Angeles Times, April 30, 1992, https://www.latimes.com/local/california/la-me-all-4-in-king-beating-acquitted-19920430-story.html.

thereafter, and my children and I moved into his home on Easy St. Literally, that was its name.

In 1995, the verdict in the O. J. Simpson murder trial was handed down. I remember watching it on television along with the rest of the nation. I had predicted his acquittal based on the fact there was no murder weapon. The outcome made perfect sense to me. What didn't make sense was the clearly racial, as opposed to procedural, reaction to the verdict outside the courtroom. Why was there such great elation in the black community matched with the shaking of heads in the white community? The significance of a black man being acquitted in the criminal justice system was lost on me. Several years later, on the 30th anniversary of the Report of the National Advisory Commission on Civil Disorders Report, The Millennium Breach, co-authored by former Senator and Commission member Fred R. Harris was released. "Today, there is more poverty in America, it is deeper, blacker and browner than before, and it is more concentrated in the cities, which have become America's poorhouses," said Harris.

As the years passed, my mother's health began declining, and when the time came, my sister and I became her hospice caregivers in my home. Since my father's passing five decades earlier, I had the honor of being at the bedside end of life of many loved ones and close friends. I refer to it as an honor because it truly is, in much the same way it is an honor to attend a birth. Our mother comfortably lived out her last months in my home with fresh air, home-cooked meals, and her favorite hymns and verses. Surrounded by her children and grandchildren when she took her last breath, I placed my head on her still chest and whispered, "We were so lucky." Everyone in the room had personally experienced her vast kindness, humor, and non-judgment, and her quiet strength and faith.

The challenges of my children's late teenage years and a new direction in my husband's career meant our common interests and shared goals were growing less and less. With both of my parents now passed, new clarity and perspective came. After nine lovely years together, my husband and I parted as dear friends and remain so today. I had been in Arizona for twenty years and now felt a release from my life there and a desire to return, alone, to my native Los Angeles.

✳ ✳ ✳

IT WAS GOOD TO BE HOME again in Southern California. As destiny would have it, I found my next job at the very same community-based agency in which I had accompanied my mother four decades earlier, The Children's Clinic, in Long Beach. With the guiding principle of service deeply ingrained in me from both my father and my mother, I quite naturally assumed the familiar role of raising funds for the "most vulnerable" individuals served by the very dedicated team at the clinic. I'm sure there were ways in which I was indirectly meeting my own needs for healing within this dynamic.

My role, as is true for many development professionals, was writing private and government grant proposals, and managing a signature special event. I lived in a small apartment near the clinic, next to a vacant lot. In the apartments on the other side of the lot lived a beautiful young Hispanic girl with whom I became friends.

Together we planned, planted, tended, and harvested a community garden for several years, always accompanied by her little Chihuahua. I believe a child can learn everything they need to know about life through participating in the seasons of a garden. And this was true for my little friend. Late one afternoon, I heard her outside desperately calling the name of her little dog. When I went out to meet her in our garden the next morning, she ran into my arms sobbing.

The family found the little dog dead by the side of the road. We buried her small friend in a particular spot, beneath a tree, in the corner of the vacant lot near our garden and created a little shrine for him there. She wrote out all her feelings and placed them there along with his picture. She sat under the tree, both with me and alone, pouring out her broken heart and grief. I had my pain to share in the sacred place as well. In this particular season, I had begun a loving relationship, which had, at the age of forty-nine, miraculously resulted in a pregnancy. We were stunned and thrilled. One day while walking from my apartment to my office, I stumbled and fell forward onto the street. I felt it immediately; the pregnancy was terminating. When I returned home from the hospital, and my body began slowly recovering to its non-pregnant state, I found the time spent in prayer, and receptive silence beneath the tree was a place to heal my feelings of deep sadness and loss too.

The miscarriage drew me closer to my partner, and we decided to move in together. I got a position as a Major Gifts Officer at Cedars-Sinai Medical Center and moved from Long Beach to his home in Los Angeles. At Cedars-Sinai, I was responsible for the activities of a particular donor group, The Associates, an inspiring and genuinely caring group of private donors. At one point, the story of the brutal abduction, sexual assault, and murder of a five-year-old white child hit the local news. My heart went out for the family, and I organized an office-wide donation to send financial support. One of my black colleagues commented, as she was generously contributing to the pool, that she was saddened to hear about this tragedy, and yet wondered if I was as concerned and activated for the murder of a black child. This question caught me up short.

While my upbringing had taught me to be a helper, to be of service, it had not instilled in me a feeling of shared humanity with people of color. There had been numerous murders of little black girls of which I had been unmoved to take action. Upon really giving her question some honest inquiry, the silent answer I had to admit in my deepest heart was no. This ingrained racism was not only hard to acknowledge, but it was also equally hard to want to spend much time exploring. It was much easier to deny and ignore it. I am today deeply grateful to this colleague for posing this fundamental question directly to me. Her question was the beginning of the awareness of the unintentional, conditioned racism hidden within my own heart.

This same colleague did the fundraising for Cedar-Sinai's 39' Mobile Medical Clinic, the COACH for Kids. The program started in 1994, as a mobile medical and case-management program providing free primary and preventive healthcare services for low-income and medically underserved children and their families in Los Angeles County. It operates under the belief that a healthy child does not exist without a healthy family and offers social services assessments, plans, and referrals. Working alongside my colleague to help create funding for this critical program kept me involved in underserved communities. After several years with the fantastic Community Relations team at Cedars-Sinai in Beverly Hills, I was motivated to find a job at ground zero of the Los Angeles homelessness crisis — Skid Row. This decision was primarily informed by my conditioning that the way to fight racism and poverty was to help black people. The hypocrisy within the words to "help the less fortunate" underscores the unlevel playing field that creates and perpetuates this class distinction.

* * *

I TOOK A POSITION as Director of Development at one of the many social service agencies. My job was to conclude a $25 million capital campaign for a newly completed facility in which residents of Skid Row could find shelter and help.

The first week in my new job, I received a phone call from a trauma center nurse notifying me, as emergency contact, that a loved one had been severely injured in a stabbing incident. My ears started to ring as the nurse explained how the wounds were so severe an Air Evac had been called. How the knife had punctured a lung causing it to collapse, a pneumothorax. And I finally heard her say they had pulled through and their life had been saved. Recovery for my loved one was slow and difficult and there were many setbacks. And there was a criminal trial to face. When the time came, I attended the hearings. When the defendant appeared, the person responsible for causing such pain and suffering to a person I loved, I experienced a flush of both anger and fear. And I noticed how easily these feelings extrapolated to the race of the attacker, a person of color. It was nearly tribal.

During this same time, I was working to settle into my new job in the heart of Skid Row.

For anyone unfamiliar with the realities and scale of Skid Row, it is home to thousands of individuals experiencing long term homelessness, drug and alcohol abuse, untreated mental health conditions such as schizophrenia, bipolar disorders, major depression, and arrests and recent release from incarceration. This downtown area is a stone's throw away from Men's Central Jail for Los Angeles County in one direction, and the heights of Los Angeles culture in the other—Walt Disney Concert Hall, Dorothy Chandler Pavilion, Ahmanson Theater, and Mark Taper Forum.

There are a plethora of services and service providers in Skid Row, and yet it remains the same: Los Angeles' shame. From my office on Skid Row, the specter of the nearly windowless Twin Towers Correctional Facility was a pervasive backdrop. Los Angeles County jail system is the largest in the U.S., with about 20,000 detainees. Fifty-year-old Men's Central houses about 5,000 detainees, most awaiting trial, having not yet been convicted. Each day, and more often each night, it disgorges its detainees out onto the streets. The geographic proximity of Skid Row to Men's Central Jail, with its massive population of men of color, seemed at least an equally significant factor in the racial demographics of Skid Row. The U.S. has the highest incarceration rate in the world and is the only democracy in the world with no independent authority to monitor prison conditions and enforce minimum standards of health and safety. Working in Skid Row brought me right into the belly of the beast. Personally and professionally, I was experiencing the realities of the criminal justice system as both the prosecution and defense.

In her book *Post-Traumatic Slave Syndrome* (2005), Joy Degruy writes of a visit to speak to a group of incarcerated young men, sixteen to eighteen years old, at Riker's Island where the inmate population is 85 percent black. "I wondered how many Americans were aware of this island penitentiary that housed multitudes of nameless black people. And if people were aware, why was there no public outrage? Here the word *overrepresentation* is the grossest understatement that fails to account for so blatant a wrong."

In a *Los Angeles Times* article the chaotic conditions at the Barry J. Nordoff Juvenile Hall were described including shattered windows, smashed walls, and overwhelmed staff. One of our local Christmas caroling groups sings at "Juvy" during the holidays. It is a strange paradox to attempt to bring cheer into this dangerous, dysfunctional, and enraged youth detention facility. Perhaps, similar to many social programs, the effort does more for the givers than the receivers. (Stiles 2018)

The racial disparities in U.S. jails and prisons start here in the juvenile system. According to the Prison Policy Initiative, the three major injustices common with the adult system are: unnecessary pretrial detention; incarceration for the most minor offenses; and glaring racial disparities (Sawyer 2019). While black children make up only 14 percent of U.S. children under eighteen, 42 percent of boys and 35 percent of girls locked up are black. A myth-busting podcast, *Complicating the Narrative*, created by and from youth, sheds important light on the loss and trauma experienced in violence riddled neighborhoods. These are important voices to be heard.

In Los Angeles, a Probation Reform and Implementation Team (PRIT) was formed in 2018. The team was charged with synthesizing hundreds of recommendations, contained in multiple reports and County audits, into an integrated, comprehensive reform plan, with timelines, metrics, performance indicators, and desired outcomes as a Probation Systemic Reform Plan. Their recommendations were unveiled in August 2019 which included plans for a permanent new civilian oversight panel. Community-wide support of a 2020 ballot measure empowered this panel to ensure comprehensive criminal justice reform and implement alternatives to incarceration. This is a hopeful sign that perhaps, in addition to the downstream issues of overcrowding and recidivism, school problems, economic problems, or a home life with physical and substance abuse need equal attention and resources at least. It's a tall order, as it could be said the correctional system is the warehouse for all our race problems.

Los Angeles County Jail is said to be the largest mental health facility in the nation. When the psychiatric hospitals were closed in the 1960s, thousands of individuals experiencing serious mental health conditions were released out into the community with a bag full of medications. Community-based service providers were supposed to receive and support them, but there weren't enough to match the need. The unintended consequence was that many of those vulnerable individuals lived out the rest of their days on the streets. Individuals experiencing long term homelessness, such as this, are the highest utilizers of the most expensive emergency healthcare services. Beyond the moral imperative, the cost of this ineffective solution continues to tax payers at a great expense in public healthcare resources.

It is often said Skid Row is the result of a broken public mental health system. But if serious mental health conditions cut across all socioeconomic, racial, and ethnic lines, why are the long term residents of Skid Row primarily individuals of color? While there is some diversity of age, ethnicity, and gender among the short term residents of Skid Row, most of these individuals have come across hard times and addiction and move through homelessness comparatively more quickly. It is among the residents experiencing long-term homelessness that the demographic skews to individuals of color. A fundraising colleague in Skid Row commented that a client reported he didn't want to come for services in the brand new $25M facility. Its sizeable open sleeping areas, bunk beds, and aluminum mirrors in the public restrooms reminded him too much of Men's Central. I was stunned. This same colleague also asked me, "How come it's always a white hand helping a black hand in the promotional material?" This simple, honest question made me realize just how deeply enculturated was the white savior/black victim narrative in me I hadn't, before that moment, given it a second thought. I had a lot to unlearn and reframe.

These realizations and questions were akin to what Victor Hugo might have meant when he described "an idea whose time had come." I can best illustrate this a by paraphrasing a parable popularized in the 1930s by social reformer and community organizer Saul Alinksy:

> "A group of campers on a river bank who are just settling down for the evening when one of them sees a baby in the river. He immediately dives in, braving the fierce current, and rescues the infant. But as he climbs ashore, one of the other campers spots another baby in the river in need of help. Then another. And another. Overwhelmed by

the sheer number of babies, the campers grab any passer-by they can to help them. Before long, the river fills with desperate babies, and more and more rescuers are required to assist the campers. But they manage to mold themselves into an efficient lifesaving organization and, over time, an entire infrastructure develops to support their efforts; hospitals, schools, foster caregivers, social services, trauma, and victim support services, lifesaving trainers, swimming schools, etc. At this point, one of the rescuers starts walking upstream. 'Where are you going?' the others ask, disconcerted, 'We need you here! Look how busy we are!' The rescuer replies: 'You carry on here . . . I'm going upstream to find the bugger who keeps chucking all these babies in the river.'"

I sought to understand what might be the upstream causes of the outcomes we were attempting to improve in Skid Row. This quest soon led me from the downstream job in Skid Row to a position upstream as interim Director of Development for Western Center on Law and Poverty—California's oldest and largest legal services support center. This dedicated group of attorneys fight for justice and system-wide change to secure housing, health care, racial justice, and a strong safety net for low-income Californians. They attain policy solutions for their clients through litigation, legislative, and policy advocacy, and technical assistance and legal support for the state's legal aid programs.

I had been on the job for about a month when Hurricane Katrina hit. The lens from which I viewed the event was that of a weather catastrophe, a natural disaster. Also, as a former Realtor, I have to admit the thought crossed my mind that no one should build in a low lying flood plain. As the hours stretched into days, there was little or no emergency water, food, or medical supplies in the evacuation center at the Superdome. Citizens stood on their rooftops waving American flags, desperately looking to be rescued. Armed white law enforcement and residents blocked their poorer neighbors from crossing a bridge to the safety of their neighborhoods. In the end, at least 1,833 men, women, and their children perished in the hurricane and subsequent floods.

I began to see the callousness Katrina had laid bare. The suffering of low income Americans had taken a backseat to terrorism and the war in Iraq. National leaders were absent on vacation. The president appeared uncaring, and he was not the only one.

It was at Western Center on Law and Poverty, I became familiar with the American Civil Liberties Union's National Prison Project. In 2009, Terry A. Kupers released a report on the nightmarish conditions at Men's Central Jail, asking for sweeping improvements to its conditions. His findings fell just short of pronouncing the practices in correctional facilities as state-sponsored torture, followed by institutionalized, legalized, racial, and class discrimination for life. Particularly for individuals experiencing mental health conditions. The American Civil Liberties Union of Southern California publicly called upon the Los Angeles Board of Supervisors to review the toxic situation, abuse, and overcrowding in Men's Central documented in the report. My walk upstream led not to discovering an individual bad actor throwing babies into the river, but a deeply entrenched and complicated mix of poverty, bad schools, and a War on Drugs resulting in a school-to-prison pipeline for people of color.

It was at this time when I was objectively, intellectually, writing winning grant proposals describing the pressing needs and proposing help for the problems of individuals on Skid Row that a young man I knew very well was accused of a crime and arrested. Held in the mental health unit of Los Angeles County jail, he awaited trial for three months. I visited him weekly. I was a white woman in a sea of visitors of color in the jail's large waiting area—described as one of the saddest places on earth. I experienced the visits by telephone through the glass, the near deafening noise, and watched the steady decompensation of my friend. I also attended his court hearings, watching the overworked public defenders, the sleep deprived detainees coming and going through the rushed process like deer in the headlights, accepting plea bargains that gained a high conviction rate for the judge and prosecutors. As Michelle Alexander explains: "The pressure to plea bargain and thereby 'convict yourself' in exchange for some sort of leniency is not an accidental by-product of the mandatory sentencing regime. The U.S. Sentencing Commission itself has noted that 'the value of a mandatory minimum sentence lies not in its imposition, but in its value as a bargaining chip to be given away in return for the resource-saving plea from the defendant to a more leniently sanctioned charge.' Describing severe mandatory sentences as a bargaining chip is a major understatement, given its potential for extracting guilty pleas from people who are innocent of any crime" (Alexander 88). I was appalled and sickened.

I had joined those with lived experiences and was feeling it within my heart. I was walking a mile in their shoes.

I remember offering advice to my friend, interpreting his experience based on what I assumed he might (or should) need and want. In hindsight, I realized how disrespectful that was. Decades earlier, I had a similar experience of sending a letter to my first crush from the adjacent, not-so-white neighborhood in Lakewood, who was by then serving time in prison. In the letter, I naively shared my particular new brand of Christianity with him, in hopes of being encouraging and making a connection. I know now, I was meeting my own needs at his expense. I heard from his family later how upsetting that letter had been for him. I regret that. I later learned of his death during a race-based inmate riot while he was incarcerated.

Any mother knows the searing pain of helplessness when they are unable to protect their child from harm. Individuals and families experiencing the correctional system know the depths of this despair.

The signing of The First Step Act in December 2018, with overwhelming support from both Republicans and Democrats, would begin long-overdue steps to reform the federal criminal justice system, and with it, the hope that progress is not only possible, but underway.

Throughout my nonprofit career, I was the person whose job it was to raise charitable contributions for the continuance of the downstream safety net agencies. Through this work, I was deeply inspired, for decades, by the generosity of many caring donors. They were moved to help, with their hearts in the right place, and with moral and religious codes motivating them to contribute. Still, as a dedicated development professional, I was deeply challenged by Martin Luther King Jr.'s words that while philanthropy is commendable, we must not overlook the circumstances that make it necessary. Gary Olson, Emeritus Professor of Political Science of Moravian College, said: "The one thing that Big Philanthropy must overlook is the green elephant astride the boardroom's conference table, the economic system that causes and extends these injustices in perpetuity."[3] The words of these visionaries evoked my own inner monologue yet I couldn't speak it within my field. I was working to address the downstream symptoms of inequality while the regulatory practices, labor and wage policies, and tax structure ensured the distinct winners and losers remained perpetually the same. Close to $200 billion federal dollars are expended each year on assorted varieties of corporate "incentives," a polite word for welfare. Medicaid receives about half the amount corporations receive each year via tax breaks. Supplemental Security Income (SSI), the federal program for individuals with disabilities receives less funding than American businesses are given in direct federal aid.

In the public sector, President Lyndon B. Johnson's great society programs of the 1960s had declared war on poverty, and a world of official anti-poverty programs had developed. I had written many grant proposals to multiple jurisdictions and secured public funds for community-based programs. But I had to wonder if these economic initiatives were empowering individuals in poor communities for real upward mobility or perpetuating the status quo? As Dambisa Moyo puts it, "The problem is that aid is not benign—it's malignant. No longer part of the potential solution, it is part of the problem—in fact,

---

3.   Gary Olson, "Philanthropy: Looking a Gift Horse in the Mouth," *Common Dreams*, January 15, 2016. https://www.commondreams.org/views/2016/01/15/philanthropy-looking-gift-horse-mouth.

aid is the problem" (Moyo 2009). I knew, from personal experience, how much a little bit of help could mean when times were tough. But I couldn't imagine the disempowering effect and frustration from the steady flow of systemic assistance without the opportunity to participate in economic advancement would have. I didn't have to.

I needed and wanted my development career to be part of upstream system change as well as downstream evidence-based solutions. I left Western Center to become a nonprofit consultant in hopes of broadening my impact. For the next several years, I provided my consulting services to small to mid-sized nonprofits. It was during this time I learned consulting can be 50 percent actual work and 50 percent spinning up clients. I also learned the pros and cons of working solo. In 2008, I had an offer from one of my clients to, once again, return to an in-house position and lead a development team. I decided to take it.

In this collaboration it was stimulating to be with a group of dedicated professionals addressing both policy and programs. During my ten years on the executive staff, I learned how to successfully navigate the complex layers of private/public funding and increase my capacity for bureaucracy. I also learned to deal with ambiguity and surprises.

In the summer of 2014, near the end of my tenure, an unarmed black eighteen year old, Michael Brown, was killed by police in Ferguson, Missouri. His body lay under a sheet on the street for hours. As the rage of the black community mounted, week-long protest and riots ensued. Not unlike the Watts Riots, there was a strong militarized response.

Law enforcement is a difficult job. My former husband is a police officer, my nephew a deputy sheriff, and my cousin a retired California Highway Patrol Officer. Each of them has faced traumatic accidents and situations that continue to haunt them every day. They are personally committed to honor, respect, and accountability. Between this and my military upbringing, my first thought was there must have been procedural reasons behind the way everything played out.

Lurking in my own mind, and affirmed by a video released of Brown stealing cigars and manhandling the store clerk, was the entrenched negative stereotype of black criminality—a thug. But this time, there was public outrage at the lack of focus on the role centuries of racial injustice played in the riots. An op-ed appeared in *The Washington Post* by Carol Anderson entitled, "Ferguson isn't about black rage against cops. It's white rage against progress." (Anderson 2014) I had only a spoon-fed understanding of what kindling ignited the Ferguson flames, but surely didn't see a connection between white resentment and black progress. Could I, as a white person, be unconsciously yearning for the good old days of white superiority? And if so, could that longing possibly translate to policies undermining progress for people of color?

All of this led me to question why so much was invested in the police, and so little in education. But I had a wonderful new grandson on the way, and that was a much happier thought. ∎

Me (r) at my bridal shower with my niece (l), in Lakewood, 1973. *Carolyn L. Baker Family Archives.*

Getting ready to go to Long Beach Community Hospital for the birth of our second child in our VW van, 1976. *Carolyn L. Baker Family Archives.*

Here I am (c) surrounded by my mentors Kay Baker (l) and Mary Jane Reynolds (r), retired Long Beach Children's Clinic social workers in Joshua Tree, CA, ca. 2000. *Carolyn L. Baker Family Archives.*

CHAPTER 4

EMMETT TILL

"Bad men need nothing more to compass their ends,
than that good men should look on and do nothing."
**—John Stuart Mill, 1867, Inaugural address
delivered to the University of St. Andrews**

ONE OF MY SPECIAL FRIENDS in my Northeast Los Angeles neighborhood is an African American woman. She is a psychologist and teaches doctoral courses addressing clinical implications and treatment of trauma and collective trauma, race and racism, and wellness and healing. Each February, she graciously allows me to ask for her suggestions on meaningful books and films to take in during Black History Month. In 2016, I was sitting on my couch watching one of the recommended documentaries as the narrator began to unfold the story of the 1955 murder of Emmett Louis Till. I was stunned as the shocking photos of Till's brutalized body crossed the screen, just as they did when his mother Mamie demanded the media show the graphic images because she "wanted the world to see what they did to my baby." I turned to my partner, barely able to speak, tears welling up in my eyes. "How could I have not known about this?"

My heart was broken wide open. I experienced the immediate and universal horror and anguish any mother would feel at the sight of such cruelty to her child. The pictures of Till's brutalized body did to me what the 1963 smiling school photos of the four black girls murdered at the 16th Street Baptist Church in Birmingham had not. I looked directly, as a mother, into the face of a child brutalized beyond recognition. It could have been any mother's child. It could have been my child. As my response moved from my head directly to my heart, I felt the reality and depth of my previous complacency.

Just in case there happens to be anyone else unaware of one of the most galvanizing events of the civil rights movement, Emmett Till was a fourteen-year-old youth from Chicago brutally murdered while visiting relatives in Money, Mississippi. Emmett and his cousins were joking around at a grocery store when he made the fatal mistake of interacting with a white woman, Carolyn Bryant, violating the strict racial codes of the South. Emmett was kidnapped in the middle of the night, four days later, by Bryant's husband and brother-in-law, then tortured, beaten beyond recognition, and shot. His body was tied with barbed wire to a cotton gin fan and thrown into the Tallahatchie River. The two men responsible were caught, tried, and acquitted by an all-white, all-male jury, some of whom had participated in the crime. The two murderers later admitted to the crime in an interview in *Look* magazine. And three decades later, Bryant recanted her testimony, saying she had lied about much of the story.

Back in the 1960s, Bob Dylan had written the lyrics and music to "The Death of Emmett Till" (1962), memorializing the murder. But back in the 1960s, no one I knew was listening. I'm sorry. I'm working to listen now.

In a CBS interview that same Black History Month, Timothy B. Tyson, the author of *The Blood of Emmett Till* (2017), was asked why he thought Bryant had initially lied about the Till incident. The depth and complexity of the cultural foundations creating Bryant's white mindset means there is no quick, simple answer to this question. As Tyson pauses to begin to articulate a response, the interviewer moves on. At that moment, the realization began to dawn on me; the murder of Till is not exclusively an African American story, it is an American story that belongs to all of us. Way beyond the squeamish embarrassment of my ignorance of the event, I was sickened, horrified. The phrase "I'm free, white, and twenty-one" came back to me. The image of Emmett Till's disfigured face showed me what this casually accepted white supremacy really meant.

This dichotomy brought to mind a powerful example my mother once gave me. During World War II, she, like many Navy wives, was separated from my father by long months at sea. They were, in fact, Pearl Harbor survivors. Aboard ship, there wasn't much for the servicemen to do on payday except gamble. There were times when my father would send home more pay than she expected. And, there were times when he would send back less. "If I was going to accept the benefits of his gambling willingly," my mother had said. "Then, I'd have to accept the negative side just as willingly." It's two opposing sides of the same coin. And this is how it is with whiteness. Participating in the extraordinary benefits of white privilege also means participating in the legacy of violence, theft, and oppression of others that created it. When Mamie Till-Mobley made me look directly at the face of race hate, I felt a loss within my humanity.

I wonder what effects the soul wound of America's racial hatred has had upon the psyche of our nation, the loss of our way as human beings. Perhaps we're not punished FOR our sins as much as BY our sins. Hate has a way of punishing both the victim and the perpetrator. As Shakespeare said in *Romeo and Juliet,* all are punished. One night on the evening news, I watched a touching story of a dear man, Tony Foulds, who tends a memorial in a city park in England. The monument is a tribute to the airmen/crew killed when they couldn't make an emergency landing in an open field in which Foulds and his boyhood friends were standing during World War II. "We thought they were just waving," he said of the airmen. "Actually they were trying to tell us to get out of the way." With the kids in the field, the pilot veered away, and the Mi Amigo plane never made it over the surrounding trees. The memorial stands where the plane went down, and Foulds comes by almost every day. In the news clip, with tears streaming down his cheeks, Mr. Foulds recounts the day of the crash. He was only eight years old at the time, but today at age eighty-two, he is still visibly wracked by the self-inflicted guilt for being responsible for the deaths of the airmen. The pilot of the Mi Amigo was John Kriegshauser, and his nephew lives in Chicago. "We are very touched by his devotion and remembrance," the nephew said of Foulds. "He's as much a victim of this as were my uncle and the aircrew."

In my segregated white childhood, intellectual assent was given to the idea that racism existed in some places in America, and it was very wrong. In Sunday school, I sang the song, "Jesus loves the little children, all little children of the world. Red and yellow, black and white, they are precious in his sight." In the 1960s and 1970s, the mystical

Hindu symbol "OM," from the sacred texts of the Eastern Vedanta philosophies, adorned my posters and clothing. As a tool for meditation, it led one into the awareness of absolute oneness, behind the changing forms of the intellect, body, mind, ego, and senses. I think this oneness is what Jesus meant when he prayed, "Thy kingdom come, thy will be done, on earth, as it is in heaven" — a prayer that this oneness would be the actual lived experience of life on the planet. Or as Rodney King put it," Can't we all just get along?"

That I was unaware of the murder of Emmett Till showed me how the dominant white paradigm shaped brotherly love, mainly within its community. Peggy MacIntosh defines this cultural programming even further. "I was taught to see racism only in individual acts of meanness, not in invisible systems conferring dominance on my group," she wrote. "I have come to see white privilege as an invisible package of unearned assets which I can count on cashing in each day, but about which I was 'meant' to remain oblivious. White privilege is like an invisible, weightless, backpack of special privileges, maps, passports, codebooks, visas, clothes, tools, and blank checks. Describing white privilege makes one newly accountable." (MacIntosh 1989)

I want to clarify the white privilege to which MacIntosh refers isn't about one's earnings or status. There are plenty of white individuals living at and below the poverty line. Instead, the concept relates to privileges conferred upon members of the dominant group, to all white people, of any kind, by being white. And while the knapsack of white privilege may be invisible to us, it is not hidden to people of color. Taken even a step further, rather than talk about single racist episodes such as Emmett Till or Rosa Parks, consider that everything within the invisible knapsack of white privilege came to be through violence to people of color—the "other."

The Statue of Liberty was supposed to hold broken chains in her left hand, with more broken chains and broken shackles at her feet. The chains were symbolic of the end of slavery in the United States (Kahn 2010). But back in 1865, the financiers of the statue requested the chains in her left hand be replaced by a book, as we see her today. The artist Bartholdi, being an advocate of the figure's original purpose, left the broken shackle and chain at her feet. The chains are not visible from the ground; they are viewable only from the air. Similarly, while the shackles of the overt racial oppression of the institution of slavery is unseen, its impact is still present in the wounded soul of America and the psyche of all its citizens.

Like Tony Foulds, I was an eight-year-old when death became real to me. It is common for children to come up with a belief they were responsible for the accidental death or illness of another. Survivor's guilt is real and has symptoms similar to that of PTSD. I wonder why more hasn't been done to help heal America's collective experience of its race and class hate, a public outcry at the behaviors and systems causing such pain and loss.

The government could surely help Americans collectively heal from a history of genocide and racism by at least including the whole story in civic monuments and days of remembrance. And, taken to its natural and logical conclusion, this would include apologies and reparations to a long list of "others" from whom much, if not all, was taken. Not in the sense of individual white people writing checks to black people, which is the way I think many white people envision the concept of reparations. Instead, repayments are due in the sense of when, in 1988, President Reagan signed the Civil Liberties Act offering a formal apology to people of Japanese descent incarcerated in internment camps during World War II, paying out $20,000 in compensation to each of the more than 100,000 surviving victims. Or reparations in the form of the Marshall Plan, when the U.S. gave $13 billion in economic assistance to help rebuild Western European economies after the end of World War II. Even within my lifetime, reparations are a debt owed to black citizens by corporations, states, and the federal government for racially restricting them from a fair share of investment opportunity. While we cannot change the past and no individual, or nation, is perfect—perfection is unattainable—reparations are morally right in the twenty-first century. That is the Christian tradition of confession and repentance.

My mother had a phrase to guide my actions as a youngster, "Do it as though your life depended upon it." What if the actual survival of the nation depended upon us pulling together, *e pluribus unum,* as if our lives depended upon it? What would it take to make "we" become our actual reality in America? This real-life human unification can be witnessed, and happens quite naturally, in a shared disaster or cataclysmic natural event. In these situations, a shared agenda is the basis of the group's survival. The abstract concept that we're all in this together becomes an actual reality. Risk management practices alone would indicate the dire need to "get it together" while we still can.

There was a phrase used as a drill back in Typing class at Los Alamitos High School, "Now is the time for all good men to come to the aid of their country." It correctly fills out a 70-space line. The phrase was a variant of Patrick Henry's, "Now is the time for all good men to come to the aid of their party." I think that's an important distinction. As I write this, I'm standing in the Northern Hemisphere, and it is winter. At this very same time, someone is standing in the Southern Hemisphere, and it is summer. For the sake of our nation, now is the time to own our collective experience and include everyone's perspective. For those who say we should stop looking back regarding race, I find this odd, given our long-standing national tradition of regular patriotic days to celebrate our freedom-loving past.

The point of insight then is action and responsibility. With a more accurate understanding of whiteness comes the obligation to speak up regarding the American narrative and policy changes needed to right past and current imbalances, all year round. That we isolate February as Black History Month is, in itself, a statement that the rest of the months are not the full history of America. I'm grateful for the complete education I'm receiving from both Black History Month and the California African American Museum in Los Angeles, which has helped raise my awareness thus far. Acknowledging racial injustices from the past brings with it the responsibility of correcting embedded systems and conventions still operating today.

When I attained the requisite age of sixty-five, I received my red, white, and blue Medicare card. The timing seemed right for me to step down from my position in the nonprofit sector and sort through the depth of my cultural ignorance and denial of race and class history. I was increasingly aware I could make this change due to the decades of opportunities afforded to me by racial reference. I retreated to my small bungalow in the heart of Northeast Los Angeles, a neighborhood with a vibrant mix of races, ethnicities, faiths, preferences, genders, abilities, and incomes of all ages. That's how it looks today anyway. Not all that long ago, this area, adjacent to lovely Pasadena, barred all non-Caucasian people from homeownership by restrictive covenants to legally exclude them. Jewish people were forced to divulge their mother's maiden name. Neighboring South Pasadena, San Marino, Arcadia, Glendale, and La Cañada were all reputed to be sundown towns, where people of color were made to leave the area at dusk, our very own Jim Crow. Only servants employed by white residents could reside in these whitest neighborhoods.

It was during the first six months of my time away from nonprofits that a university admissions scandal broke, and at the heart of the story was a 501(c)(3) public charity. I was stunned that the thrust of the news story centered on the rich and famous defendants rather than on a system where payments for illegal services were tax-deductible. The abuse of the tax-exempt status resulted in a number of conspiracies, including charges of racketeering, money laundering, conspiracy to defraud the United States, and obstruction of justice. Could not these charges be leveled against any number of systems creating and perpetuating distinct lines of class separation and exploiting the poor?

I, who once was all happy, and peppy, and bursting with love, became the person who could quickly ruin a dinner party. Discovering the murder of Emmett Till made me care as a human, start reading and researching, and begin speaking out. Being aware of a more complete story of the legacy of whiteness made me not only accountable to all people of color, but also to myself. ■

Emmett Till with his mother, Mamie Till Mobley. *Collection of the Smithsonian National Museum of African American History and Culture, Gift of the Mamie Till Mobley family. ca. 1953-1955.*

The Tallahatchie River where Emmett Till's body was found. *Photo courtesy of Richard Apple, 2013.*

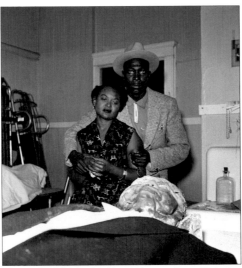

Mamie Till Mobley looking at her son's mutilated body. She insisted on a public funeral service with an open casket to expose the world to racism and the barbarism of lynching. *Time magazine, David Jackson, 1955.*

CHAPTER 5

WOMANISM

"The world will be saved by the Western woman."
**—The Dalai Lama, Vancouver Peace Summit,
September, 2009**

IN MUCH THE SAME MANNER in which I became aware of the story of Emmett Till, the documentary, *Feminists: What Were They Thinking?* (2018) introduced me to aspects of the women's movement I had missed in the 1970s.

The documentary's director, Johanna Demetrakas, shows the complexities black women continue to face trying to align with being both anti-racist and pro women's rights. Margaret Prescod (host of the radio program, *Sojourner Truth*) shares in the film how, in the 1977 Congress-mandated U.S. Conference on Women in Houston, Texas, she attempted to raise a resolution opposing the forced sterilization of black, Native American and Puerto Rican women, and her microphone was cut off. The rationale given for this by the group was because freedom of choice was the focus, and the issue needed a presentation most appealing to white men, the decision-makers. Women of color had to put their concerns and issues on the sideline for the greater good.

Many women of color refused to identify as feminists, concluding that white women had sold them down the river. "We did ask that we not be segregated into minority women, over on our own," said Carmen Delgado Votaw, Co-Chair of the National Advisory Committee on Women, voicing a similar position that diverse voices are unheard. "We wanted to be part of the mainstream of women, that we wanted to be included in every part of the plan that affected us" (Demetrakas 2018).

Across town during the National Women's Conference in Houston, a group led by Phyllis Schlafly and Lottie Beth Hobbs held a protest rally against this federally funded feminism. While the women's rights and the pro-life/pro-family movements seemed to be in opposition to one another, they were parallel in the sense that both were primarily associated with white, middle class women. Neither group fostered an equal sharing of power for women of color or had an understanding of how intersecting aspects of non-white women's identities compounded discrimination against them.

Also in the film, Funmilola Fagbamila, who has been organizing with Black Lives Matter movement since its inception in 2013, examined the complexities of black political identity. "So where then do black women exist in this conversation? Within the black space, you can't talk about your gender, and within women's spaces, you can't talk about your race. But you are both, equally, every day when you wake up. What do you then do?" (Demetrakas 2018).

It appeared white feminists had little to no interest in the concerns of women of color. Rather, women of color were asked to be allies to the white feminist's agenda. While white women only had to deal with gender, black women had to deal with both gender and race. From examples such as these, it is easy to see how the notion that solidarity is for white women came to be.

As a white woman, I experience gender inequality differently than a woman of a different race, socioeconomic status, or sexual orientation. One way to repair the disenfranchisement experienced in previous waves of feminism is to ensure powerful platforms for all women to claim their space, speak for themselves, and be heard today. Imagine the power of this inclusivity, unity, and collective support.

An example of this is the Say Her Name movement. Together we call attention to violence against black women and girls, demand their stories be integrated into calls for justice, policy responses to police violence, and media representation.

While I had the experience of thinking and talking about my gender as it pertained, for example, to equal pay for equal work, I had not had the experience of thinking and talking about my whiteness, as if I too had a race. I identified with other woman based on the unique reproduction and biological functions we shared—we menstruate, and some of us bear children. Within that, I grew up with the particular cultural constructs of my gender identity and what it means and how it looks—through clothing, hairstyle, voice, and body shape, to be feminine.

During the throes of the feminist movement of the 1970s, I was actively involved in the Peace Movement and the Jesus Movement instead. So rather than attending consciousness-raising groups and reading books such as Kate Millett's *Sexual Politics* (1970), and Virginia Woolf's *A Room of One's Own* (1929), I attended prayer meetings and read Christian literature. My marriage ceremony at nineteen was a very evangelical service, as I promised to love, honor, and obey my husband. In the meantime, women's roles in marriage, home, and family were being influenced through *The Feminine Mystique* (1963) by Betty Friedan, *The Golden Notebook* (1962) by Doris Lessing, and *The Second Sex* (1949) by Simone de Beauvoir. I, at the time, was reading literature outlining how the ideal childbearing years were during one's early twenties. I gave birth to my daughter when I was twenty, and my son when I was twenty-two. I only tangentially supported approachable feminist topics such as affordable childcare, rape crisis intervention, and equal pay for equal work. And any mainstream woman could support these issues as they were neither anti-male nor anti-Christian.

Alice Walker said, "Womanist is to feminist as purple is to lavender" (Walker 1983). In the same way lavender is a whitewashed, mild form of purple, feminism is a whitewashed form of womanism. The second wave of the feminist movement mainly represented and served middle-class white women, without special needs, who were pretty much benefiting from the patriarchal system. Women like me. From within the black community comes a term for we white women — "Becky."

While a Becky theoretically appreciates all women, she is offended by the promotion and solidarity of women of color and does nothing to uplift, praise, or respect these sisters. The Beckys of those days perhaps even furthered the profile and image of the poor, ignorant, black welfare mother. In my own life, my lack of actively advocating for women of color, as well as being a "helper" in nonprofits, puts me squarely in the Becky camp. The second wave of feminism primarily served us Beckys. In short, the Movement, as author Alice Walker said, started "taking after their brothers and their fathers. And that's a real problem."

I pause here to give gratitude, where gratitude is due. In my twenties, I was a client in a shelter program for battered women. I experienced that universal powerlessness, rage, and fear. The help of women involved in the second wave of the feminist movement were there for me. With their support, I began to take responsibility for myself. I was able to forge a new life as a single mother, complete a graduate degree, and land an executive job. As difficult as those days were, and as hard as I like to think I worked, it is also accurate to acknowledge my place within the socioeconomic shades of whiteness. I was allowed to seize opportunities such as mortgages, refinancing, and home equity advances. I was able to parlay social connections others did not have. I'd also like to add, during all of those years of undergraduate and graduate coursework in the College of Education, I was never once asked to examine the effects of the American economic and social hierarchy on people of color.

I know firsthand from this challenging chapter in my own life, somewhere along the line, we all hit a low point and need a helping hand. And what a mercy it is to receive that help. I've heard it said that people don't cry when they lose hope, they cry when they find it. I have known this experience. My motivation in the context of the feminist movement during the 1970s and 1980s, was mostly, if not wholly, self-serving. My climbing the corporate ladder and breaking the glass ceiling wasn't about challenging the patriarchal system. It was about finding a way I could benefit from it to look out for myself and my young family. I was able to make my way into the economic system, played well with others, and invested in my children and community. In the late 1990s, a significant health crisis with one of my children drained all the resources I had.

I now know just how fortunate I was to have had those resources. I also knew, along with all mothers, the universal heartache of watching my child suffer, and knowing I couldn't protect them. I'm not sure whether I was oblivious at the time to the additional challenges mothers of color were facing, pretended they didn't exist, or didn't have the emotional bandwidth to take on one more thing as a single mom. Maybe it was a combination of all three.

So, do I identify with the women's movement today? It was with this question in mind that I visited www.womens-march.com and read the evolving policy platform defined there outlining "the structures and systems perpetuating discrimination in the U.S.", in preparation for attending the 2019 Women's March in Los Angeles. I took the metro train to the march to see what the posters were saying, what the younger women had on their minds, and to get the tone of my local community.

On the way, I met two white women, both about my age, both executives in nonprofits addressing affordable housing, as I had been. As we traveled, we reflected on the different waves of the feminist movement. We appreciated when the suffragettes (from the late 1800s to the early 1900s) succeeded in gaining the right to vote for white women in 1920 with the Nineteenth Amendment. We each had come of age during the second wave during the 1960s and the 1970s, and were in solidarity against Vietnam, working for passage of the Equal Rights Amendment (ERA), and reproductive rights. And how, in the third wave of feminism in the 1990s, we had championed parity, gender equality, individualism, and diversity in our careers. And now, social media was defining the fourth wave of feminism with the #MeToo movement.

We talked about how, in hindsight, we had to acknowledge the feminist movement had been created by white women, for white women, and catered to white women. And how, in contrast, the deliberate inclusion and conscious honoring of women of color is now well reflected in the nineteen Unity Values and Principles of the Women's March. Today's intersectionality-infused policy platform and Unity Principles for the Women's March include the voices of diverse groups of women, and their multidimensional life experiences have been listened to, respected, and reflected. Yet the color divide has prevailed.

One of the Unity Principles declares, "We believe it is our moral imperative to dismantle the gender and racial inequities within the criminal justice system." My time visiting in and working around Men's Central created strong feelings about the prodigious need for prison reform, so this one piece of the march's agenda is enough for me to say I'm in, I want to join this conversation.

Here's the rub: I see a similarity between this Unity Principle and that of "Opening Doors: Federal Strategic Plan to Prevent and End Homelessness." The Department of Housing and Urban Development's plan is dependent upon what's known as the Coordinated Entry System, the operational component of any community's effort to end long term homelessness. Seventeen bulleted points outline the values and qualities of the Coordinated Entry System. Ten bulleted points describe how to access the process. It is a massive, nationwide, comprehensive plan to accomplish a critically needed humanitarian and economic goal. However, when an individual experiencing long-term homelessness passes successfully through each of the sequential coordinated steps and finally reaches the last stage—moving into permanent supportive housing—the process stagnates and, at times, comes to a grinding halt.

Why? Because there is no appropriate supportive housing unit available for them. News flash! Ending long-term homelessness is dependent upon the availability of affordable permanent supportive housing units. In like manner, and as stated in the Unity Principles, dismantling the gender and racial inequities within the criminal justice system is dependent upon one thing—a shared moral imperative. There needs to be consensus, based on data, as to what programs and institutions are creating and perpetuating the school-to-prison pipeline. And that dismantling and reforming these inequities will take an agenda shared by conservative and liberal positions. A shared vision and agenda is the real moral imperative and is, in fact, our responsibility and patriotic duty.

It is precisely this lack of a shared agenda that causes women of color to have raw and real emotions about white women. Women of color are not responsible for fixing a system they did not create, and one from which they do not benefit. Thus it is the responsibility of white women to take on this agenda and make things right. And great care is needed in attempting to repair the deep divide between women of color and white women.

But in order for a conversation to be appropriate and safe for any willing participants, great care and skill must be devoted to creating both the set and setting. There are some existing rubrics, such as Critical Friend Conversation Protocol and others, guiding individuals in exploring an essential question, challenging their assumptions, and coming up with a strategy to address the question. But before even approaching processes such as these, an understanding of the historical and psychological relationship between black and white women is a critical prerequisite, and a thorough understanding of the underlying concerns. It goes without saying that preparation and knowledge are key necessary components before even broaching these tough, stressful topics. This is the work for white women, not women of color, to do.

While at the 2019 Women's March, I also spoke with a white mother and daughter who had a sign "ERA now" and who described themselves as "weak activists." When I asked the mother why she felt that way, she said: "We aren't doing all that much in our daily lives." I think this may be the way some white women feel today, not knowing what work is still needed. Some suggestions on examples of ways white women can "do the work" are offered in the Anti-Racism Checklist on p. 167 at the end of the book.

I believe part of the problem is more white women need to publicly show up as allies as race issues arise, whether it is the police shooting of an unarmed black man, or verbally responding to and calling out racism among white people. I am curious why a younger generation of women is not eager to identify as feminists today. They are speaking out and showing up, opening doors, and breaking down barriers. I would like to hear their perspective.

My mother's approach to her catastrophe was to reach out with an open heart to do something for someone else in need. She was the master of fun and silliness, practical jokes, and handmade surprises. Preparing and launching all these antics took her thought and time. I remember driving around Lakewood Gardens delivering gifts of May Day baskets, homemade Valentine's Day cards—every seasonal holiday occasion—to the homes of people she thought might be uplifted by them. These were times when she wasn't thinking about her own misery. Givers gain.

Another woman's life that had a significant impact on me was Peace Pilgrim. On January 1, 1953, the year I was born, Peace Pilgrim started walking along with the Rose Parade in Pasadena and kept right on going, eventually arriving at the United Nations' building in New York. Printed on the back of her blue tunic were the words "25,000 Miles on Foot for Peace." She carried with her only a comb, a folding toothbrush, a ballpoint pen, copies of her peace message, and her current correspondence, which a friend would forward. Her goal was to carry the message of peace, and she said, "I shall be a wanderer until mankind had learned the way of peace, walking until I am given shelter, and fasting until I am given food." She walked without any money and was not part of any organization. She walked "as a prayer." After completing the 25,000-mile trek in 1964, she continued to walk. It was a twenty-eight-year pilgrimage for peace in which she crossed the U.S. seven times (Peace 1992).

What inspires me about Peace Pilgrim, born Mildred Norman, is her awakening to a deep sense of connection to the world around her, to everyone. She relinquished her individual identity and felt herself part of the flow of all experience rather than just an observer of it.

✳ ✳ ✳

ALL AMERICAN WOMEN have experienced sexism, it comes with the patriarchal territory. In like manner, as a white woman growing up in American culture, I have benefited from the structural advantages of whiteness. The trajectory of privilege allowed me to find myself in the center of opportunity. It has been said to whom much is given, much will be required. So in this way, my goal is to listen, to open doors, to provide support and mentorship, be an ally, and both give to and receive nurturance from other women.

As a female professional, I've been surprised and saddened, not so much by how I was treated by male colleagues, but by how my female colleagues often tore one another down. There is a sense of scarcity, of competition, as if it is a zero-sum game. Scarcity theory might lead young girls to believe that there are limits around how many good things can happen to any one person, which could also lead them to believe that their own success will be limited (Miller 2017). Women and girls would benefit significantly from training on how to build empowering friendships and to uplift each other.

There are many books and films to be found in A Mighty Girl's extensive collection of girl-empowering resources. Founded in 2012, A Mighty Girl is the world's largest collection of books, toys, and movies for parents, teachers, and others dedicated to raising smart, confident, and courageous girls. The material is multicultural in scope, addressing girls from different ethnic backgrounds. For example, a fantastic guide for girls on building healthy friendships is "A Smart Girl's Guide: Friendship Troubles" for ages eight to twelve. For an excellent guide for teen girls, thirteen and up, try "The Teen Girl's Survival Guide." There are also books to help kids learn how to be a good friend at every age in the blog post, "Making and Keeping Friends: 60 Mighty Girl Books About Friendship." And social media is a potent channel for women to acknowledge other women's substantive achievements, rather than their physical appearance. When women connect and see each other as allies rather than a threat, only then will we be able to support each other and achieve our self-determined goals.

The purpose of this hard-won gender equality is that my words and actions might be helpful, impactful, and of service. I believe it is my responsibility today to ask women what disparities are they experiencing, and what I can do to be of support, to be an ally. And then to respect the answer. My goal today is to strike a healthy balance between collective well-being and my well-being. I was raised on this quote that has been attributed to John Wesley:

> "Do all the good you can,
> By all the means you can,
> In all the ways you can,
> In all the places you can,
> At all the times you can,
> To all the people you can,
> As long as ever you can."

A crucial component in this poem is the phrase "as you can." I'm not called upon to do more than I'm reasonably able. I'm also the one responsible for my self-care—getting adequate rest, eating good food, having fun, and exercising. A longtime friend, raised in the Jewish tradition, once shared a Midrash story with me about Rabbi Simcha Bunem of Pershyscha. The Rabbi is said to have spoken about carrying two slips of paper, one in each pocket. The words on one slips reads, "For my sake the world was created." The other slip reads, "I am but dust and ashes." These two messages suggest a balance as we walk through life. Sometimes I naturally spend more time in one of these two mindsets and would do well to look at the other, as needed.

All the Big Problems are not solved. And everyone is going through something. Your child is born with special needs. A beloved family member dies. You have an accident or illness that suddenly takes away your ability to live independently. That is life—it is as fragile as it is fierce. I have two hands – one for helping myself and one for helping others. And, as I have two ears and one mouth, I am to listen twice as much as I speak.

Some ways I advocate for women include: supporting women-owned businesses, particularly women of color; calling and emailing my elected officials on women's issues; cheering for another woman's opportunities and accomplishments without constraint; seeing where my jealousy of other women is an indication of where I could be doing more with my own life; and contributing my creativity and imagination to the vibrant and diverse young girls and women within my sphere.

Maybe it's the old hippie in me, but as I saw in the spiritual awakening of the 1960s, impermanence is an undeniable and inescapable fact of human existence from which nothing that belongs to this earth is ever free. The nature of life is change and flow. Womanism is recognizing and respecting the human capacity for healing, growth, and transformation—both for myself and for others.

Twenty years ago, the Dali Lama said Western women would save the world. He inherited his compassion from his mother and believes women have a nurturing instinct and can better empathize with those who suffer. Empathy and compassion are traits that can prevent humankind from destroying itself, and they are cultural rather than racial or ethnic traits. Perhaps this is the essence of both the Dalai Lama's statement and womanism—the emphasis is on our natural contribution.

Because of all the progress made by women who have gone before and upon whose shoulders we stand, I find myself in a place of opportunity and empowerment. Women have overcome oppression and traditional roles and made enormous progress towards equality. I have the freedom to act. Now with partnerships, listening, learning, and conversations, I can better understand what is not working and how to address those issues while respecting local needs. I don't think it's too far of a stretch to say it is women who will save the nation.

I have several vintage quilts handmade by my great-grandmother and grandmother. Back in their day, several generations of women would sit together at the quilting loom, and create these treasures. The dynamic within these gatherings of women was depicted in the 1995 film, *How to Make an American Quilt,* based on a novel of the same name by Whitney Otto. The story tells of a young woman visiting her great-aunt and grandmother as she thinks over a recent proposal of marriage. While there, she encounters eight women of a quilting circle working on a free-form, crazy quilt. As she becomes aware of the differing experiences and identities of these women, the young woman gains insight into her own life choices.

Contemporary versions of these quilting bees are being held every month in New York, Los Angeles, and San Francisco, minus the actual quilting. Led by a community host who is a member of WeAreQuilt.com, these gatherings are ways women are meeting for topic-driven conversation, action, and support along the journey. I believe projects such as these come out of a cultural need, particularly at this divisive time, for women to communicate what is disturbing them and participate in the diverse wisdom, empowerment, and inspiration among us.

As a lover of quilts and textiles, I attended Adia Millet's Breaking Patterns exhibition at the California African American Museum. It was a glorious collection of miniatures, photographs, and textiles. Of her work, Millet says, "In our lives we are given situations, we're given a piece of fabric, we're given a space, and have opportunities to shift them into something else. We can create something more beautiful out of something decaying. The material is just a way to take whatever we have and create something new. The human experience, the history behind the fabric, the memory that it evokes in its viewers, can take it in multiple directions. Which is why, oftentimes, I try to get materials that we don't always imagine together and put them together so that we can see that our identity and our existence is much more complex than just one fabric."[1]

Right now, women of differing races, identities, and experiences have the opportunity to shift, to get together. The Say Her Name movement is a prime example. Together we call attention to violence against black women and girls, demand their stories be integrated into calls for justice; policy responses to police violence; and media representation. We have the opportunity to break the previous patterns of separateness, and create something new and more beautiful out of decay. That is Womanism to me: making my natural contribution, in ways I haven't always imagined, for the wholeness and well-being of all. ∎

1.   "Adia Millett: Breaking Patterns," California African American Museum (CAAM), 2019, video, 1:00, https://caamuseum.org/exhibitions/2019/adia-millet-breaking-patterns.

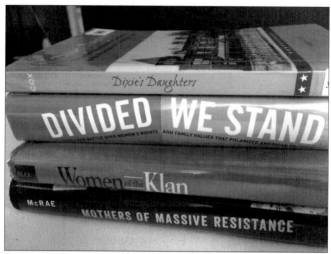

Some of the books I have read on the role of white women perpetuating racism in America. *Carolyn. L. Baker Family Archives.*

Women of the Ku Klux Klan (WKKK) at KKK services, 1925.
National Photo Company Collection/Library of Congress Catalog.

Me and my mother, Mary Louise, when I received
my Bachelor's degree from Arizona State University,
Tempe, 1981. *Carolyn L. Baker Family Archives.*

At the Clinton Global Initiative
in New York, 2010. *Carolyn L.
Baker Family Archives.*

Hands of the helpers in Santa Monica, ca. 2012. *Carolyn L. Baker Family Archives.*

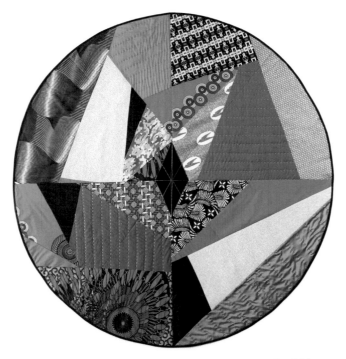

"Medicine Wheel" from Adia Millett's "Breaking Patterns" exhibit at the California African American Museum (CAAM) in 2019. *Photo courtesy of Adia Millett, www.adiamillett.com.*

CHAPTER 6

IDENTITY GROUPS

"Me against my brother; me and my brother against our father; my family against my cousins and the clan; the clan against the tribe; and the tribe against the world." **—An old Arab Bedouin saying**

O NE OF MY PET PEEVES while working in nonprofits was the prevalent use of the label "the homeless." All those working with me could testify this term was stricken from our spoken and written word. I referred everyone to the Americans with Disabilities Act (ADA) guidelines: "Put people first." The appropriate order of the words in a sentence would then be a person experiencing homelessness. First and foremost is the person, an individual, then the condition. There is a wide variety of individuals experiencing homelessness; it is not a homogeneous group.

Back in the 1960s and 1970s, women, gays, and blacks organized within their identity group for liberation. Individual members of each of these oppressed groups could gather together, share everyday life experiences, build important political and social activism, and create a proud and positive self-identity. Immutable characteristics, the kind of things measured in demographic information, are the basis of many identity groups. The problem with identity politics occurs when mutable characteristics such as religion, economic status, education level, political party, ethical views, etc., are also assumed to be shared by all the individuals within an identity group.

If I resist anything today, it is putting my ideas and passions in a box with a label on it. Or that my life would be interpreted for me by anyone else. It follows, I would now work hard at not explaining what's going on in anyone else's life, or offering advice on what to do about it. And even if I were able to resolve problems for others, they would remain stagnant.

Looking back on the multiple identity groups with which I've associated through the years, I can't help but think of the book *Psycho-Cybernetics* (1960), Maxwell Maltz's classic self-help book, which basically asserts you can't outperform your self-concept. Throughout my life, I've found groups that matched my inner attitudes and self-image, and then internalized the goals of that group. The overstimulation of an identity group, such as a religious or political culture, creates a definite closed-mindedness and stereotyping of any outsiders opposing the group-think. And having conversations mostly within a group reinforces the pressure to conform and show group loyalty. Follow all this to its natural conclusion and it's easy to see how a group identity progresses to polarization and standoffs, making inter-group communication impossible.

In 1957, Carl Rogers and Richard Farson coined the term "active listening." They wrote: "Active listening is an important way to bring about changes in people. Despite the popular notion that listening is a passive approach, clinical and research evidence clearly shows that sensitive listening is the most effective agent for individual personality change and group development. Listening brings about changes in peoples' attitudes toward themselves and others; it also brings about changes in their basic values and personal philosophy. People who have been listened to in this new and special way become more emotionally mature, more open to their experiences, less defensive, more democratic, and less authoritarian."

During my unraveling first marriage decades ago, we went to a therapist that utilized Active Listening. Each of us had to fully concentrate, understand, respond, and then remember what was being said by the other. This process was time-consuming and took courage, patience, and humility. In short, it took being an adult, something we both lacked at the time. The childish communication style of today's differing political identity groups reminds me of those days, gaining an advantage as the primary objective. There was a 1990s version of this active listening process as well, described by Tom Rusk with D. Patrick Miller in *The Power of Ethical Persuasion: From Conflict to Partnership at Work and in Private Life* (1993). This version added communicating how the other's thoughts and feelings affected you, essential when intense emotions and defensiveness can derail communication. This version included agreeing to disagree and to go your separate ways while still respecting the other.

Is there any reason for hope when there seems to be an intractable divide between identity groups? According to the researchers at The Difficult Conversations Laboratory at Columbia University Teachers College, the answer is "yes." They found when the pre-existing narratives of participants were expanded by exposure to the complexities of an issue, they were more thoughtful and open to considering the perspective of "the other" during a conversation. And it appears even international rivalries can be successfully worked out through a process of compromise and negotiation.

In my work with government jurisdictions and in presenting at public town halls, I have seen the way the decision-making methods of identity groups can affect outcomes as well. There is an excellent contrast in the group decision-making process between the failed Bay of Pigs Invasion, which had a disastrous result and was costly in lives, and the group decision-making process of the Cuban Missile Crisis, which potentially saved us from nuclear ruin. In his commencement address at American University in 1963, President Kennedy urged Americans to reexamine Cold War stereotypes and myths and called for a strategy of peace that would make the world safe for diversity. "For, in the final analysis, our most basic common link is that we all inhabit this small planet. We all breathe the same air. We all cherish our children's future. And we are all mortal." Being an ally in making the world safe for diversity calls for reexamining stereotypes and identity groups. Making the world safe for diversity means seeing myself as neither less than or better than my fellow human beings. And I, as an individual, am left to address the thing I might have wished to avoid — working to improve myself, the content of my character.

Several years ago, since it was my professional goal to interact with and listen to the community, I decided to check out Hi From the Other Side, an organization that pairs friendly people across the political divide to talk like neighbors. Not to convince, but to understand. It's an impressive effort to humanize people as individuals, particularly concerning identity politics. This from www.

hifromtheotherside.com: "Do you feel there's too much name-calling in political discussions? Do you find the words and actions from the other side of the aisle alienating? If this sounds like you, sign up here or follow our newsletter. Once we find a match, we'll shoot you two an email introducing you for a one-on-one conversation."

When I filled out the online registration form, it asked me three personal questions: "What did you want to be when you grew up? How did you come to that idea? Other comments? My answers were: What I wanted to be when I grew up was a medical doctor. I came to that idea because, in my young mind, a doctor seemed to be the one with the most power, knowledge, and the compassion to help people. Then, when Hi From the Other Side finds someone who wants to discuss the same issue as me, they'll send me and my match an email and leave it up to us to find time for a call or video chat. They even have a conversation guide to help us get started.

The idea is to get to know each other as people. In my comments, I said I'd like to have an open-minded one-on-one conversation concerning prison reform, reparations, immigration, the war economy, school vouchers, or ecological devastation. But first both sides must read up on the complexities of both sides of the issues. Then, through the honesty of having sensitive and difficult one-on-one conversations with a real person, we might both recognize more human likenesses than differences. We might give or receive a surprisingly kind word or a helpful suggestion of actual benefit. We might find something admirable in the other, something to be respected. And in this open-mindedness, even if uncomfortable, state my long-held notions could be explored. When it comes to addressing much needed systemic reforms, one thing I've noticed about the difference between one identity group and another is sometimes merely the speed of the design, roll-out, and implementation of the solution. Imagine!

There can be real fear in launching a frank discussion on race relations. For example, recently at a rural high school, a fight broke out in the restroom involving white male students and the one and only black male student. In addition to the physical assault, the altercation involved disgusting racial epithets. Rather than bring the event into a public forum for a powerful teaching moment for the students and community, the event was handled privately, behind closed doors. I make no excuses for the code of white silence and maintaining the status quo. Yet, I do understand and acknowledge how white culture is bereft of language and is deeply unskilled in having honest conversations about racism.

This is where the guidance of a Charette Procedure can be of great help. The procedure enables a large group of people to think about an idea together, everyone participates, and all are helped to form an opinion. Depicted in the film, *The Best of Enemies* (2019), a Charette Procedure, employed by Bill Riddick, helped the deeply divided community of Durham, North Carolina navigate a school integration vote in 1971 with a very surprising outcome. And it was the realization of deeply held human pain, understood and shared by both sides that led to an awakening.

To progress, this self-denial by God-fearing, patriotic, all American communities must be disrupted. A vocabulary and skills to participate in discussions about whiteness are both needed and wanted. And, in parallel, the courage to be less afraid to use them.

Several years ago, during Holy Week, *La Semana Santa*, I was out in my garage, and I heard the sound of tires screeching followed by a thud. It was the kind of sound one hears and immediately knows something terrible has just happened, but not knowing to what degree. With a feeling of great dread as to what I might find, I ran from my garage out into the street. About 50 feet away, a small crowd was gathering around a young man who had been struck by a vehicle while riding his bicycle. One helper was on his cell phone calling for emergency help; several others crouched over the young man, speaking his language, yet another was directing traffic.

I saw myself hurrying into the midst of the situation and confidently commanding, "Step aside; I'm a doctor!" The odd thing about this vision, of course, is that I'm not a doctor. This glimpse into my imagined position of a savior made me stop and shake my head at myself. The young man was, in truth, surrounded by the right helpers and, thankfully, was soon rising to his feet.

As for me, during this week reflecting on transformation, death, and resurrection, I was reminded of the Rudyard Kipling's poem, "The White Man's Burden" (1899) and the call of Empire to humanize the non-white world. Of believing the white race is morally obligated to rule the non-white peoples of the planet by encouraging their economic and social progress by "civilizing" them, displacing their native cultures. "Step aside, I'm a doctor!" How utterly false this imagined superior and manifest destiny! I can also see how this trait also shows up in relationships with family, neighbors, and colleagues. I've got to get over myself.

From my mother's side of the family, I inherited my second great-grandmother Lydia Baldwin's handwritten memoir, written in 1897, chronicling her Quaker life on the Indiana frontier in the 1800s. Her stories describe protecting slaves running to freedom beneath the floorboard of her safe house and peaceful relationships with the indigenous people of the region, inviting them into the family's home for a meal. I read of her unique personal joys and hardships, and the universal losses, such as the death of her beloved young son, as they made their way into new unknown territory. Her youngest child Lucetta Baldwin, my great-grandmother, married and came West in the 1880s with her husband and three boys to a mining camp in southern Arizona.

My imagined account of their lives and times has comprised the historical fiction I've been writing for quite some time. But beyond the hagiography of the rugged individuals and brave pioneers is the critical factor of mobility allowed to them because they were landowners, thanks to the Homestead Act of 1862, which subsidized racially restrictive land grants. Other landless families, in those early days, faced extreme poverty and devastating hardship.

About the same time California was honoring the Fugitive Slave Act, another one of my distant pioneer ancestors, Elias "Lucky" Baldwin, was hiring available black workers for multiple projects, including building Santa Anita Racetrack. Some of the workers became very successful jockeys. The financial literacy and prosperity of his workers helped make Baldwin Hills one of the most affluent black communities in Los Angeles. On this same maternal side of my family, I remember a curio cabinet in which my grandmother's collection of "pickaninny" dolls was carefully displayed.

My father's side of the family comes from Clay, Leslie, and Perry Counties in Appalachian Kentucky. The hardship of abject rural poverty was the catalyst for him and his brothers to enlist in the Navy at very young ages and stay there. According to my older siblings, my father used to read us the Little Black Sambo stories, supplying the voices of the characters in a black minstrelsy dialect. My white ancestors who came before me, on both sides, were a mix of lower and middle classes, none from power or wealth. Nancy Isenberg explains how class and power distinctions were, and are, as much at the heart of injustice as is race. Changing the balance of this embedded power structure, how we hate and punish the underclass, would be among our nation's most significant advancement and accomplishment to date (Isenberg 2016).

Humans are 99.9 percent the same genetically. In 2000, J. Craig Venter, in heading up the Human Genome Project put it this way, "Race is a social concept, not a scientific one. We all evolved in the last 100,000 years from the same small number of tribes that migrated out of Africa and colonized the world."[1]

For example, when my two children check the Caucasian box, it represents a mix of English, Irish, Welsh, Italian, Mexican, Cherokee, Spanish, French, and Portuguese — that we know of, from recent times. Each race box is a mix of all the other boxes. There is but one actual collective group — those of us breathing the same air and inhabiting the earth.

With my insular upbringing as part of the dominant group, it never occurred to me that I, as a white person, even had a race. But I unconsciously knew a lot about the

---

1. Natalie Angier, "Do Races Differ? Not Really, Genes Show," *The New York Times*, August. 22, 2000. https://www.nytimes.com/2000/08/22/science/do-races-differ-not-really-genes-show.html.

social facts of whiteness, and within that space, race is genuine and persistent. Evolution being what it is, my white identity at twenty, forty, and sixty has reflected my cultural milieu, lessons learned, and those still underway. It is fluid. And as a human, I am continually vacillating between behaving in a good or bad manner.

Back in the hippie days, there was a particular collective look and feel to "doing your own thing," so much so that the recognizable style is a party theme today. A vital evolution I see today is I have the agency to choose the group or groups with which I identify, how I do or don't socialize, and in what collective processes I involve myself. I carefully consider the complex issues of today, and my position on one doesn't predict my opinion on another.

Similar to putting "people first" as suggested by the Americans with Disabilities Act (ADA), it is a given that individuals within any identity group are just that, individuals. It is here I want to make clear the distinction between the artificially constructed identity group known as the white "race," and whiteness. As a fair-skinned Anglo person, I check the "Caucasian" box as a way of identifying myself as part of the white race. Whiteness, however, is the normative privilege granted to me as part of the white race. Importantly, this whiteness exists only in relation to and in opposition to "other." The difficulty to form and articulate an answer as to why Carolyn Bryant lied under oath at the Emmett Till murder trial illustrates the depth of the insidious paradigm within America's white psyche and culture. And the knee-jerk response to preserving it.

As the saying goes, you can't choose your parents. But as a member of the white race, I can choose how I relate to whiteness. I can choose to continue passively participating in whiteness and its benefits, and maintaining the status quo. Or I can choose to try and give words to it, make it visible, resist it.

I had an experience several years ago at a bustling and congested gas station. As I pulled up to the pump and started to get out of my car, an African American woman pulled up very close behind me and angrily yelled out her window, "You think you're the only one that matters!" She then threw her car into reverse, backed up, and went around me. I looked up to realize there was an available pump in front of me that I was blocking. Her rage, her perspective, was like a punch to my gut. It blew me right out of the comfort that "I'm okay, I'm one of the awake and aware, one of the good ones." This experience was my first encounter with a black person's anger against not only a culture of white superiority, but against me personally. I directly experienced the "other" relationship to whiteness.

Back in my high school choir days, I learned and performed a song to what is known as the Prayer of Saint Francis. It was a beautiful arrangement:

> "Lord, make me an instrument of your peace
> Where there is hatred, let me sow love
> Where there is injury, pardon
> Where there is doubt, faith
> Where there is despair, hope
> Where there is darkness, light
> And where there is sadness, joy"

This song and its inspiring and uplifting lyrics are still with me today. They are here at my writing desk. Similar to Shakespeare, these words have exact relevance in today's world. They come back to me as often as I seek, through prayer and meditation, to improve my conscious contact with God as I understand him/her.

So what does it mean for me to be an instrument of peace today? I believe it means I need to become more fluent in the "language of resistance" to whiteness. As Tim Wise succinctly put it in *Speaking Treason Fluently* (2008):

> "If whiteness is to be undermined as a dispenser of privilege and advantage—in other words if we are to create a society of justice in which one's skin color or continental ancestry is of no consequence in determining one's station in life—one must learn the vocabulary of resistance, just as surely as one has previously been taught the vocabulary of collaboration."

Furthering my fluency in the language of resistance is a way of putting people first. It requires not only being able to see the perspectives of others, but to speak up, to break the code of silence. Doing otherwise is remaining complicit, against which I want to be vigilant. Even more importantly, fluency in the language of resistance means reframing the narrative, the lie that people of color need help as a result of racism. No. Through the process of reviewing my own white history and identity, I see "the problem" lies within a long standing racial and class hierarchy. But how to separate from a group culture that has been embraced for so long? Awakenings such as these are not usually based on logic, but rather from a disruption, such as the one I had when I looked at the face of Emmett Till. Before that I didn't relate to images of racism. I could remain indifferent.∎

My barefoot forebears in Appalachian Kentucky,
ca. 1900. *Carolyn L. Baker Family Archives.*

My siblings and I (r) at our parent's gravesite in Fort Rosecrans
National Cemetery, Point Loma, CA, 1999. Carolyn L. Baker Family
Archives. *Carolyn L. Baker Family Archives.*

Displaying the flag on my front porch, every day of remembrance. *Carolyn L. Baker Family Archives.*

CHAPTER 7

THE ILLUSION OF SEPARATENESS

"The role of the prophet is to bring to public expression
the dread of endings, the collapse of our self-madness,
the barriers and pecking order that secure us at others
expense and the fearful practice of eating off the table
of a hungry brother or sister." —**Walter Brueggemann**

IN THE 1960s, eastern philosophy awakened me to how
Western culture constructs the world as a collection of
disparate "things." In contrast, the natural world is interre-
lated, connected in a fluid, dynamic way. Experiencing the
literal reality of this oneness is a common feature reported
by individuals taking psychedelic drugs. The illusion of separateness is at the root of the ineffective ways in which we
relate to politics, business, and each other. This idea made
me wonder then, is it nature or nurture that creates how we
view and experience race relations? Because of my childhood, nurtured as I was in a white community, I felt different
from people of color. And the notion of being a good person
and "helping" people of color was deeply ingrained in me.
But what role does human nature itself play?

There is a human phenomenon, schadenfreude, in
which we experience joy from observing the suffering of
others. Schadenfreude means your failure represents my
improvement or validation. And it's not enough that I win,

it is equally important that you lose. Schadenfreude shows up in the hardwired, unconscious position that I am different from you. Schadenfreude permeates race relations and identity groups. An iconoclastic illustration of this oh-so-human phenomenon is Bob Dylan's folk-rock song "Like a Rolling Stone." For younger readers unfamiliar with this musical reference, another example of shadenfreude is the feeling you get when you win an item in an eBay auction—you not only win the item, you also beat out those other losing bidders. It is very convenient to point to the missteps of others, to gloat even. Given this natural human proclivity, is there even a way to move toward a more holistic manner of being?

Author Rich Benjamin notes that as America becomes more racially diverse, more whites are moving to a "Whitopia," the whitest of locales. Benjamin, a black man, rented homes and temporarily became a resident of three of the fastest-growing predominantly white communities in Utah, Idaho, and Georgia. But this was less about the interactions between blacks and whites; his experiment was more about the phenomenon of white flight itself—white people moving out of a neighborhood because people of color are moving in (Benjamin 2009).

Benjamin finds the same degree of residential and educational segregation that existed back in the 1970s still vexing the nation three decades later. And this trend of racial separation continues today, along with the social and political implications of white flight, in our increasingly multicultural nation. Most Whitopians said they move to these segregated neighborhoods for friendliness, comfort, and safety. Taken to its next conclusion, these qualities are subconsciously associated with whiteness.

So what is the difference between being a white suprem-acist and being a white separatist? As one white separatist explains, "We don't think we're better than you; we just want to be away from you."

I've lived in predominantly white communities for most of my life. In Whitopias such as these, social niceties shield white people from having uncomfortable conver-sations among themselves concerning race, or looking deeper and connecting with the realities and pain of racial inequality. Then in mixed racial settings, social barriers stop white people from confronting conscious and uncon-scious biases for fear of saying something that would make us look bad, or be hurtful to a person of color. What then is the most effective means for white people to ask the questions we're afraid to ask? Where can we examine white social conditioning and patterns of privilege? How to ask another white person about institutional racism, or explore ways we hold ourselves back, or succeed at the expense of everyone else? There are white people who have already worked very hard on these topics, and are listed in the Bibliography. They are much further along than me when it comes to talking about racism, separately and in racially mixed groups. You can follow them and learn. You can also talk to me and join me on this journey. The onus is on me to do this work and liberate myself.

Similarly, do black people need and want to be away from whites, to have their own spaces? Back in the 1960s, a friend of mine was the only white person at a Nina Simone concert at The Troubadour on the Sunset Strip in Los Angeles. When Simone noticed his presence, she stopped the show and refused to continue until "the white boy" left the room, which he did. On a similar note, there is a night club in Los Angeles with a longstanding black clientele. When a friend and I went there for a night of dancing, we were the only white people in the place. No issue was made of this, except for a feeling I had that we were inserting ourselves into a black space, that we were intruding. From this I could see how Simone's action that night at the Troubadour could be less "turnabout's fair play" and more about protecting and valuing a space for people of color, a place for healing and being free from the dominant white culture. Rather than an act of racial discrimination, more like a response to it (Blackwell 2018).

✳ ✳ ✳

WHEN I BECAME the hospice caregiver for my brother John in 2017, I experienced how uncomfortable and confusing confronting whiteness can be. When our father passed away in 1961, I was eight years of age, and John was fourteen. From that day forward, my brother's style of relating to me was one of aggression. I now know this to be schadenfreude. For him to feel better, he needed for me to lose, to suffer. This difficult dynamic continued between us even into our adulthood. But towards the end of John's life, the ravages of diabetes took its toll, and he required dialysis every other day. After five years of this, and a steadily decreasing quality of life, he decided he had enough. He made the decision to stop dialysis and naturally pass away. Although it was a surprise to many people, given our antagonistic history, it was a natural decision by both of us that John would come to my home for end of life care. The arrangements were made, and July 4, 2017, was his last day of dialysis.

During the twelve days that followed, I cooked all of the favorite family meals John hadn't been able to enjoy for so long, we played his favorite music to which he heartily sang along, and we held hands and talked. We openly shared our pain and long-held grief. Acknowledging the shared loss we had each experienced as children, the sadness we each understood so well, deeply healed us. My sister joined in and penned this tribute to our father: "Thank you for a legacy of the importance of gallantry, honor, service, citizenship, neighborliness, family, pageantry, courage, going above and beyond, patriotism, devotion, marriage, and love."

There is an old cliché, "the candle burns brightest just before it goes out." One aspect of John's last days that completely stunned me were the horrific racial slurs he hurled directly at his black and brown caregivers. I had never heard him speak such ugliness in all my life. I know my parents would never have stood for this. Was this the dark place within the white psyche where conditioned hatred lives? Or maybe one final show of schadenfreude before the lights began to dim? I don't have these answers, but there it was—virulent racism, unmasked. When John's body life came to an end and he passed away peacefully, his daughter and I experienced the next revelation. Call it absolute consciousness, God, or peace—whatever one chooses—it became abundantly clear that underneath the very distinct personalities, differences, and wounds, of the body life, there is only love. I've been blessed to be at the hospice bedsides of many loved ones as they passed, and I have experienced the reality of this transcendence. Just like the Human Genome Project told us, we are one.

✳ ✳ ✳

WE ARE A COUNTRY of immigrants and diverse peoples. The concept of oneness then isn't for us to be alike, blended, and homogeneous. Neither is it to suggest we have had the same experiences or perspectives. Nor for individuals to stop enjoying nearness to those who share their particular culture, language, and customs. One of the things I dearly love about Los Angeles is its rich multicultural diversity. A quick search of area restaurants brings a plethora of its intriguing and unique ethnic offerings. *Viva la difference!* But the proverb "birds of a feather flock together" describes a safety in numbers approach to lower the risk of predation. In a social setting, the principles in the U.S. Constitution and the Bill of Rights are supposed to create that collective safety net. *E pluribus unum.* These protections—not based on race, religion, or class—are the right of every citizen.

Arguing against mob violence and lynching, Abraham Lincoln declared in his 1838 Lyceum speech that the Constitution and the laws of the United States ought to become the "political religion" of each American. And Martin Luther King Jr., in his 1955 speech to the crowd at the Holt Street Baptist Church after Rosa Parks refused to relinquish her seat on a Montgomery city bus, pronounced that justice should be based on moral principles. And that if the Supreme Court and the Constitution of the United States were wrong, then justice is a lie. The dissonance between our civic religion and our social reality is the white brokenness Michelle Obama referred to in her 2019 Obama Foundation Summit appearance – the soul wound of a broken moral backbone.

I remember one episode on the television show *Bonanza* back in the 1960s, "Strength in Numbers." Little Joe has plans for a project and wants to accomplish it alone, in his way. He pridefully pushes away the experience of others. Pa uses a bundle of sticks to illustrate a lesson. To paraphrase, he hands Joe a bundle of slender sticks and tells him to break it. Although Joe tries and tries, he can't break the bundled sticks. Pa then pulls a single thin stick out of the bundle and breaks it with ease. "Together, we can't be broken," said Pa. "Don't let pride get in your way." This advice holds for navigating the complications and intersections of race in America today. Collective liberation from racism requires white people to express a genuine vulnerability and a willingness to learn.

At the bicentennial celebration of the Constitution in Philadelphia, Sanford Levinson, professor at the University of Texas Law School and author of *Our Undemocratic Constitution: Where the Constitution Goes Wrong (And How We the People Can Correct It)* (2006), proposed a thought experiment. He asked attendees to imagine being a signer of the Constitution today, with whatever reservations there might be, knowing what we know now. "Signing the Constitution commits one not to closure, but only to a process of becoming," suggested Levinson. "And to taking responsibility for the political vision toward which I, joined I hope with others, strive." Taking responsibility for race and class discrimination is today's much-evolved version of Kipling's *White Man's Burden* (1899). It's up to white people to civilize ourselves and do the work of understanding social justice issues. When I'm stunned by yet another awareness of whiteness, it's not the burden of people of color to make me feel better. Asking people of color to help white people learn about race is another aspect of privilege (Blackwell 2018). It's up to me to do that work and create openings for real, honest conversations.

Every strategic plan I've ever written started with the vision statement, and everything else flowed from there. A vision, imagination, is the tool for recreating and remodeling systems. In August 2019, *The New York Times* ran a series entitled The 1619 Project. "The goal of The 1619 Project, a major initiative from *The New York Times* that this issue of the magazine inaugurates, is to reframe American history by considering what it would mean to regard 1619 as our nation's birth year," *The New York Times Magazine* editors declared. "Doing so requires us to place the consequences of slavery and the contributions of black Americans at the very center of the story we tell ourselves about who we are as a country."

I commend *The Times'* commitment to re-educating its readers. The 1619 Project redefined our history by shining a light on the evil of slavery, and how we defended and tolerated it for so long. And how bias, stereotypes, and systemic racism has gone unnoticed by much of the white community. Re-examining the story of the founding of the nation is a chance to see it anew, and to reframe it. Hopefully this look backwards informs our way forward. In the retelling of *all* our history, it's crucial that everyone and everything be included, and in the right proportion.

The 1619 Project is critical in that everything is connected. The Dixiecrats, the Southern strategy, all are the unfinished business of slavery. Speaking at the inauguration of President Clinton, Maya Angelou said, "History, despite its wrenching pain, cannot be unlived, but if faced with courage, need not be lived again." Until the issue of slavery and its basis in white superiority is courageously dealt with, the racism in the white psyche, and in the external structures that follow, will remain.

From Los Alamitos High School, a substantial percentage of us went on to careers as educators and in the nonprofit sector. I think this was about a belief in the power of the human spirit to imagine something and work to create it. We all grew up with Disneyland as our neighbor. In the opening scene of the trailer for the Disney docuseries, *The Imagineering Story* (2019), we hear Walt Disney say, "There's really no secret about our approach. We keep moving forward. We're always exploring and experimenting. We call it 'Imagineering'."

One of the most creative approaches to reframing the conversation on race and interrupting the narrative of extremism I've heard comes from Theodore Johnson, Senior Fellow at the Brennan Center for Justice. "National solidarity could force declaring racism a crime of the state against the citizenry, and as such, the state is responsible for the remedy. It reframes racism from a white infraction of the rights and opportunities of people of color to one where the state is culpable. This shift moves the divisive debate of responsibility out of the citizenry and into the social contract space between the state and the public. In a political sense, it pronounces the whole of the American public has been exposed to the crime of racism and adversely impacted, to widely varying degrees" (Johnson 2008). This is but one example of imaginative and practical ways to build strength in numbers, even a national solidarity, around anti-racism today.

Segregation was a system of oppression designed and maintained by white people. In 1896, the *Plessy v. Ferguson* decision established that different facilities for blacks and whites was valid under the equal protection clause of the Fourteenth Amendment as long as they were equal.

This doctrine of separate but equal legally codified racial segregation, and with it, white supremacy. It was not until *Brown v. Board of Education* in 1954 that the Supreme Court overturned *Plessy v. Ferguson* with Chief Justice Earl Warren stating the ruling deprived equal protection under the law guaranteed by the Fourteenth Amendment. Immediately after this ruling, the "Southern Manifesto" called to unite white politicians and leaders in a campaign of new state laws and policies to prevent public school desegregation.

The Black Lives Matter movement of today calls out that black citizens are still experiencing something other than equal protection under the law. The voices of the Black Lives Matter movement are to be listened to and believed. For a white person to object to, or write off, the Black Lives Matter movement stating "All lives matter!" is to miss the important outcry that black lives are still being deprived of the guarantees of the Fourteenth Amendment. Guarantees white people have always enjoyed.

In the macro picture of separateness —the individual nation states —the federal law is similar to a parent who says "no" - no state can deprive any citizen of life, liberty, or property without the due process of law. Demanding equal application of the Fourteenth Amendment throughout the land is but one example of we're all better off when we're all better off.

Today, my desire for unity includes acknowledging confusion about the pros and cons of separateness. A prerequisite for true inclusiveness requires a great deal of soul searching and self-reflection on my part. Without this personal work, inclusive settings are simply a replication of the status quo with several more people of color present. The dominance of whiteness prevails (Blackwell 2018). ■

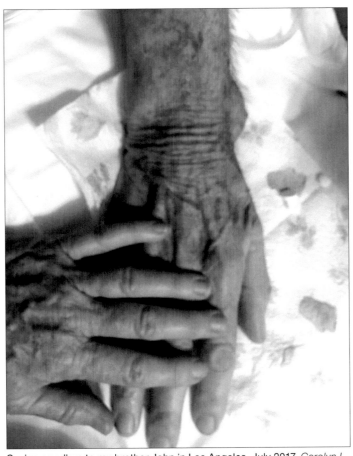

Saying goodbye to my brother John in Los Angeles, July 2017. *Carolyn L. Baker Family Archives.*

CHAPTER 8

The 11th Commandment

"This is the crime of which I accuse my county and
my countrymen, and for which neither I nor time nor
history will ever forgive them, that they have destroyed
and are destroying hundreds of thousands of lives
and do not know it and do not want to know it.... It is
their innocence which constitutes the crime." —**James
Baldwin, The Fire Next Time (1963)**

THE ORIGINAL WORKING TITLE of this book was *The
Innocence Which Constitutes the Crime.* The title
permutated several times in attempts to make it more
compact, as well as to remove the reference to crime,
knowing that would lessen the likelihood of white people
reading the book. I wish to include the quote here as a sort
of Coda, a concluding section to extend the theme of previous chapters. This powerful quote from Baldwin carries
within it the reason for my need to carefully examine my
history: "to discover what I do not know about whiteness
and what I do not want to know."

I've wondered why I reacted so strongly to learning of
the murder of Emmett Till, and why the story continues
to haunt me. The murder was a horrific act of racial violence, so that's a given. And yes, as a mother, the sight
of Till's body broke my heart. But it's been through the

reviewing of my own history as a white woman I believe I've found the reason the story still resonates. It is because of the central role Till's white accuser, Carolyn Bryant, played. In 1955, Bryant was a southern white woman living in Mississippi one year after the *Brown v. Board of Education* decision. Bryant's father managed a plantation, and her store customers were mostly sharecroppers. In response to the *Brown* decision, Virginia Senator Harry F. Byrd had created a plan for "Massive Resistance" to this forced desegregation and the plan was strongly embraced in the South. It would follow that, in Mississippi, Bryant and her husband were participants in this Massive Resistance. Part of Bryant's mainstream life as wife, mother, and storekeeper would also have included perpetuating segregation and racial distance. Or more straighforwardly, white supremacy.

It was not until I read several books on the Massive Resistance that I understood the degree to which white women were at the center of this movement (Blee 2008). I know from my own life, whenever I became involved in an identity group they got not only me, but my children and husband as well. In addition to their regular daily lives, the Bryants were likely also making sure white supremacy survived. Along comes an "uppity black boy" who doesn't seem to know his place, or follow Jim Crow. Emmett Till makes direct contact with Carolyn Bryant, who becomes the arbiter of his fate. She tells a fabricated story of having been touched and insulted by this black boy. There is conjecture she just wanted to get her husband Roy to help out more with the store and the kids. Others feel she knew full well there would be bloodshed. I can't get inside her head, but it's clear the launch of the brutal savagery begins with

Bryant. This answers for me the question as to why she lied on the stand. Her false testimony portrayed her as a good white woman, not someone capable of killing a black child. In her perjury, she maintains the white narrative, the frame.

Bryant was a woman of her times. I am a woman of my times. But no one gets a hall pass for being of their times. The relevance of Bryant's story is in the powerful role white women have played, and continue to play, in influencing their families and communities. White women make up a massive voting bloc that overwhelmingly throws its support behind conservative male candidates. In CNN polling, the divide between black women voters and white women voters is too deep to be ignored. For example in the 2018 Georgia Governor's race, an estimated 75 percent of white women voted for Brian Kemp, with 97 percent of black women supporting Stacey Abrams. In Texas, 60 percent of white women voted for Sen. Ted Cruz, with 94 percent of black women backing Beto O'Rourke. The outcomes were similar in Florida's Governor's race, with fifty-one percent of white women voting for Ron DeSantis, and eighty-two percent of black women voting for Andrew Gillum.[1]

In Bryant's time, overt racist tropes were accepted. In my times, coded racial speech is accepted. Some contemporary examples include: inner city; state's rights; illegal alien; welfare; food stamps; and law and order. These terms are ways in which white superiority is normalized. The Massive Resistance movement to uphold racial distance is not over, it is has been simply refined. Jim Crow is now James Crow, Esq.

---

1. Michelle Ruiz. "Why Do White Women Keep Voting for the GOP and Against Their Own Interests?" *Vogue* magazine, November 8, 2018, https://www.vogue.com/article/white-women-voters-conservative-trump-gop-problem.

To reiterate the words of Martin Luther King Jr. in 1968, "We must come to see that the roots of racism are very deep in our country, and there must be something positive and massive in order to get rid of all the effects of racism and the tragedies of racial injustice." (King 1968) White women actively participated in the first Massive Resistance with the goal of perpetuating whiteness. I propose the positive and massive "something" of today is women warriors taking the lead and doing the hard work of bridging the divide and saving the country from racism. Women know what it is to be mothered, and to mother. Some of the things mothers ideally want to impart to their children include: love; emotional health; wisdom; physical health; purpose; spiritual health; a passion for learning; happiness: good friends; and hope. These are the same qualities needed in our nation. America needs mothering, sistering, and grandmothering.

As a child, my mother would drive us down from Lakewood to visit my father's gravesite at Fort Rosecrans National Cemetery, just down the hill from Cabrillo National Monument in Point Loma, California. She made sure his grave was decorated every holiday—a Christmas tree, an Easter basket, and Valentine's Day hearts. I remember walking down the orderly rows reading the names, branches of service, and wars listed on the individual white marble headstones. My mother told me later in her life she had just wanted to make sure I didn't forget my father. Not a chance.

Both of my parents are buried at Fort Rosecrans. The somber view of the vast Pacific Ocean from there is a familiar sight for me. As an adult, I once volunteered to be part of laying Christmas wreaths on the graves of all those buried at Fort Rosecrans. On the appointed day, I first laid wreaths on each of my parent's headstones, and then walked to my assigned section — the men and women who had served in Vietnam. As I and the other volunteers respectfully placed each wreath, we said the name of the deceased person aloud adding "Thank you for your service."

As I moved slowly through my assigned rows placing wreaths and honoring names, an immense sadness came over me. I found myself adding the words, "I'm so sorry." These were the names of my peers, the hopeful young men and women of my generation. I felt not only the loss of life of these names, but over 50,000 more. As my tears fell, I also felt grief for how Vietnam changed all of us who remained. The broad cynicism and sharp polarization has been deep and long-lasting. The emotional wreath-laying experience I had at Ft. Rosecrans was strikingly similar to my reaction when I looked into the face of Emmett Till. How could this brutality have happened?

Early on when writing *An Unintentional Accomplice*, the United States government was shut down for a historic thirty-five days due to a bitter political standoff over a border wall and immigration policy. Deeply drawn party lines over the nation's "values" and its civil religion made communication impossible. As a friend of mine once said, "Whenever I hear the words, 'it's the principle of the thing,' I know we're all about to lose." Placing ideals over human life creates scenarios in which we can justify unthinkable brutality and even murder.

As I neared completion of the book, the nation entered an impeachment inquiry. Amid great national divide, the dichotomies of the American narrative were heartbreakingly real. One suggestion from my Twitter feed was to make sure to contact my representatives and let them know how I felt and what I wanted. Let's see, what was my Congressional District again? And which chamber—the House or the Senate—should I contact concerning my thoughts on impeachment? It had been a long time since my high school civics lessons. The point being, I had grown complacent about communicating with my elected officials concerning issues of importance. I had abdicated the power of my voice and became a bystander. Was it because I had lost faith in the democratic process?

In a time when national polarization is at an all-time high, the other part of the quote by Baldwin figured prominently in my exploration: "they have destroyed and are destroying hundreds of thousands of lives." It is fairly straightforward to examine how black people have been and are hurt by white supremacy. My exploration became more complex as I become aware of how racism has also harmed white people too.

I once visited Cuba with a group of musicians. The guide on our tour bus was insightful and entertaining. He explained the complexities of Cuba with this example: if you visit for two weeks you feel you could write a book about Cuba; if you remain for six months, you might be able to write one chapter about Cuba; and if you stayed for one year, you would find it hard to write even one paragraph about Cuba. Such it is with complex issues.

Things are not as black and white as they seem, or they may not even be at all what they seem. In exploring and sharing the stories of my lived experiences I can only speak for myself, I don't represent a class of people or political party. These are the stories of the world I grew up in, of how I came to the views I hold. Within that exploration, the three main topics that emerged for me were: the white bubble in which I existed; witnessing first-hand the systemic perpetuation of race and class disparities; and the divide between white women and women of color. I've opened these explorations in the spirit of David Susskind's *Open End* interviews of the 1960s.

We embrace the remarkable, beautiful Constitution and the Bill of Rights. We have yet to fully embrace genocide and racism as part of our national anthem. This dissonance is ingrained in the entirety of the American experience. Our country's founding is based on two dissonant ideational roots: the high and lofty values of the Declaration of Independence and Constitution set in the realities of colonialism, genocide, and slavery. Could it be our resulting mindset is the defense mechanism needed to manage our cognitive dissonance? For example, a belief that poverty is deserved. Or Trayvon Martin, Dontre Hamilton, John Crawford, Dante Parker, Tanisha Andersen, Akai Gurley, Tamir Rice, Rumain Brisbon, Jerame Reid, Tony Robinson, Philip White, Eric Harris, Walter Scott, Freddie Gray, Eric Garner, Sandra Bland, and Michael Brown probably deserved what they got, for one reason or another. And that Colin Kaepernick's protest is unpatriotic and disrespects the flag and veterans who have served to defend our nation.

And on that last note, my lifelong compliance with the U.S. Flag Codes gives me the confidence to loudly object to the outrage over Kaepernick taking a knee during the playing of the National anthem. Kneeling or not standing during the National anthem does not disrespect the flag. Patriotic outrage would be much better placed on the way the U.S. Flag Codes are routinely disregarded, and the flag of our nation disrespected, each time it is displayed flat, used in advertising, and/or in clothing. And this happens daily. Kneeling, rather, is a humble Christian posture, one of respect. As a child of the 1960s sit-in's and marches, I see this peaceful protest as a way to draw attention to bigger moral, spiritual, and ethical questions. The act of kneeling is to patiently ask our collective conscience "When will we all be equal in the eyes of the law?" Taking a knee is not done out of irreverence for servicemen and women, but with a heart full of love for America. It is real patriotism.

In his book *Stride for Freedom* (1958), Martin Luther King Jr. stressed the need to "get back to the ideational roots of race hate, something that the law cannot accomplish." When experiencing cognitive dissonance, one must either change an aspect of one's view or deny its existence.

Further complications arose when I considered how much of what I think and do might be unconscious, driven by mental processes of which I'm not even aware. The metaphor of the snake and the rope is instructive: You enter your dimly lit bedroom and see a peacefully coiled snake. Immediately your body reacts in fear. You scream and visualize the snake's strike. All this happens in milliseconds. When you compose yourself and muster the courage while hiding behind the wall, you increase the light. And there lies an unintentionally-placed rope. You see that it's not a snake and your fear vanishes. But, before you had the awareness it was actually a rope, the snake was very real and the fear very genuine. From where did the conditioning come to instinctively fear a snake, with no deliberation? I'm no brain researcher, but it would seem unconscious fears are factors in stereotyping and discrimination as well.

If all this exploration amounts to anything it is this: The cognitive dissonance within the American narrative also exists within my psyche. As conversations get confusing, it is helpful to bear in mind a quote by the poet Rainer Maria Rilke, "Be patient toward all that is unsolved in your heart and try to love the questions themselves, like locked rooms and like books that are now written in a very foreign tongue. Do not now seek the answers, which cannot be given you because you would not be able to live them. And the point is, to live everything. Live the questions now. Perhaps you will then gradually, without noticing it, live along some distant day into the answer."[2]

In fundraising, the notion of a "stop and think" gift (Sturtevant 1997) illustrates the difference between an annual gift—a contribution that can be painlessly made by writing out a check to support a cause at the end of the calendar year—and a major gift, with a significantly higher dollar amount based on a deepening relationship to the purpose. The donor is asked to stop and think about what degree of impact they would like to be making. In this same spirit, it's my time to "stop and think" about whiteness and my commitment to resisting it. Writing serves as both a penance for whatever harm I may have caused, by commission or omission, and a prayer for conciliation. Exploring my relationship to historical and current racism brings a broader understanding of how complacency equals acceptance of discrimination.

In the Midrash rabbinic legend of the two disparate slips of paper in opposite pockets, I see the dichotomy of

2.   Rainer Maria Rilke, *Letters to a Young Poet*, trans. M.D. Herter Norton (New York: W. W. Norton & Company, 1993).

living with two realities: I am but dust and ashes versus the world is created for my sake. Navigating my whiteness and guilt is a complex and sensitive process that has only just begun. It is painful as well as enervating to awaken to the reality that, no matter how seemingly unintentional, by my silence, I play a complicit role within a system that continues to inflict racial harm. By not actively opposing discrimination, as a white person, I act as an accomplice.

In a legal context, in order to be convicted as an accomplice to a crime, one must have demonstrated intent. If one unintentionally becomes involved in a crime, and takes action to notify authorities in an attempt to stop it, they cannot be charged with being an accomplice to a crime because they took direct action to not assist its commission in any way. In this example, I find myself unable to unsee my unintentional involvement in the crime of racism. With this it is my duty to move through useless guilt. It is my moral obligation not to let naiveté, embarrassment, or lack of information prevent me from participating in real conversations about race for fear of making a mistake.

I realized the seriousness of this when I listened to an interview with long time civil rights activist and singer Henry Belafonte, one of a handful of people still living who were part of Dr. King's inner circle. He said the solution lies with white Americans regaining what he called a "moral course of history." Until then, he said, nothing will change and America will self-destruct. "The case is that we have to fix it," Belafonte said. "The fact is that it's not fixable if white folks don't decide to change their course of conduct. The only thing left for Black people to do is burn it down," he continued. "We have been lynched, we've been murdered. And if you look around, never before in my 91 years of history as an American have I ever seen the nation more racially divisive than it is at this very moment."[3]

On Holocaust Memorial Day (HMD) in January 2020, I watched a BBC broadcast of a ceremony commemorating the 75th anniversary of the liberation of Auschwitz-Birkenau. There were about 200 survivors and their families present along with several thousand visitors. The event was themed around the phrase, "Stand Together." The chief executive of the Holocaust Memorial Day Trust, Olivia Marks-Woldman, said of the anniversary, "identity-based prejudice and hostility is worryingly prevalent in the UK and internationally."[4]

One of the Holocaust survivors at the commemoration was Marian Turski, deported to Auschwitz as an eighteen- year-old Jew. In his speech, Turski shared that, when asked how such an unthinkable thing could have happened, he explains that it starts when the idea that stigmatizing a group of people becomes normalized. And when we believe wrong science, such as eugenics. And when we see others as different, alien. In closing, Turski passionately urged the world to adopt an 11th commandment: Thou shalt not be indifferent. He said: "Do not be indifferent when you see . . . historical lies . . . when you see that the past is stretched to fit the current political needs

---

3. Charlayne Hunter-Gault, Interview with Harry Belafonte. "Harry Belafonte on realizing MLK Jr.'s dream." *PBS NewsHour,* April 6, 2018. https://www.pbs.org/newshour/show/harry-belafonte-to-realize-martin-luther-king-jr-s-dream-white-america-needs-to-change-course.

4. Mathilde Frot, "BBC to broadcast ceremony marking 75th anniversary of Auschwitz liberation," *Jewish News,* January 5, 2020. https://jewishnews.timesofisrael.com/bbc-to-broadcast-ceremony-marking-75th-anniversary-of-auschwitz-liberation.

. . . do not be indifferent, otherwise you should not be surprised when another Auschwitz crashes down on us."

Democracy depends upon the rights of minorities being protected. As another survivor at the ceremony, Elza Baker, wistfully put it, "when minorities have to feel vulnerable again, I can only hope that everyone would stand up for democracy and human rights."

Irishman John Philpot Curran said in 1790, "The condition upon which God hath given liberty to man is eternal vigilance." In that spirit, I'm moving from being a "helper" to being an ally who both acknowledges my position and seeks to provide active support for those who live with a different set of circumstances. I'm reassessing my support system, ideas, and relationships that have served their purpose, and I've outgrown. The three principles I'm following are: be open to guidance; be courageously honest and vulnerable; and be humble to know I don't have the answers. I know I have a lot to learn, and I'm taking the responsibility to do so.

As a writer I find it magical the way characters refuse or demand to come forward and face their issues. And I draw inspiration from the power of the protagonist, the one who will stop at nothing, or at least not be deterred for long from accomplishing their goal. The protagonist has to make a move, take action, get off the dime, or we lose interest in their story. It was through this observation, I began to learn to be more of a protagonist in my own life and times. Eldridge Cleaver had this to say about the writing process in *Soul on Ice* (1968). "After I returned to prison, I took a long look at myself and, for the first time in my life, admitted that I was wrong, that I had gone astray—astray not so much from the white man's law as from being human, civilized. . . . my pride as a man dissolved, and my whole fragile moral structure seemed to collapse, completely shattered. That is why I started to write. To save myself."

There is also much to learn as a reader, watching characters make decisions and face their fears in a beautifully crafted novel. The works of Shakespeare are great self-help books, with all the wisdom about the human condition contained therein. In like manner, I've heard it said: "music is what words wish they could be." How ubiquitous it is for an opera to move us to tears as the universal human themes we recognize so well—pain, joy, love, jealousy, rage, pride—are expressed sonically. And when we sing together, we have the unique opportunity to experience oneness through formless sound.

Several years ago, I was working at a nonprofit in Santa Monica, and the city was launching its public transportation system—The Big Blue Bus. A contest was being held for an opening artistic act for its Summertime Twilight Concert Series, on the pier, to promote the use of public transit. I dreamed up lyrics to a handful of popular 1960s songs, making them about riding the bus—a singing commercial of sorts. I submitted this idea and, lo and behold, got the gig. Every Wednesday night after work for the next six weeks that summer, an ever-changing group of stellar Los Angeles musicians became The Blue Notes, and up onstage at sunset, we would go. One week, Joan Baez was the headliner. In the outdoor backstage area, there she was—the person who had shaped not only the social conscious of my youth but that of an entire nation of young people. She was as beautiful as ever. After much hesitation, I decided to approach her. She very graciously welcomed me and listened with a smile as I was able to let her know how much her music and life had meant to me. How I had sung her songs to my babies. How moved I had been by her version of Woody Guthrie's song "Deportees" and its relevance today. I stopped short of inquiring her thoughts on the lyrics of "The Night They Drove Old Dixie Down," coming from the Confederate viewpoint, as it does. I stopped because the words to me had always created empathy regarding the deep pain of the Civil War period. It was neighbor set against neighbor, brother against brother. All mothers on both sides cry when they lose a son to war.

Among ways to find peace is to confront the past. While activism can be scary and off putting, storytelling has the power to heal. To move forward on my journey, I've traveled backwards to tell my story, and explore what it feels like to realize things never were what they appeared to be. And to be emboldened to question, to step forward, and speak up. I've always gravitated to things that had meaning to them. Today, a regular practice of meditation and inquiry encourages my evolving self-awareness. This is my counter-cultural revolution—one of the spirit and ego-busting. I remember a time when the phrase "It's a free country" was widely heard. This freedom is the power of ordinary people to effect positive transformation in myriad ways.

As I've shared experiences from the decades of my life in these pages, the underlying search to understand myself, my role, my place is apparent. Spirituality is always at the center of this inquiry whether it be my Quaker ancestry, fundamental Christianity, or a sojourn in India. Peace Pilgrim said, "I felt a complete willingness, without any reservation, to give my life—to dedicate my life—to service. 'Please use me!' I prayed to God. And a great peace came over me. I tell you it is a point of no return; after that, you can never go back to completely self-centered living" (Pilgrim 1983). It was surprising to Peace Pilgrim that many lives were not similarly dedicated. I vividly remember praying this same prayer, and perhaps this book is a part of the reply.

Through the written, spoken, and sung words, I see both the illusions and realities of my culture. I think this sort of disruption is among the primary purposes of the arts. Step 12 in the book of Alcoholics Anonymous says, "When a man or woman has a spiritual awakening, the most important meaning of it is that he has now become able to do, feel, and believe that which he could not do before on his unaided strength and resources alone. He has been granted a gift which amounts to a new state of consciousness and being."

I hope I have updated my position as a mature white woman amid a world of racial trauma. The end game, though, can't be to try to establish me as one of the good white people, even if only within my own heart and mind. And I must also acknowledge the ease with which I can take a break from this discomfort. Instead, may I continue to give voice to the language of resistance to racism and absolute love and forgiveness. May I offer my skills in building a more humane culture of wholeness, respect, and peace. May I work powerfully to confront the contradictions of the American dream. These actions are a vital part of the healing process and what love looks like today.

Of equal importance is the healing power of laughter. I grew up with the *Reader's Digest* and always enjoyed the very funny section *Laughter is the Best Medicine.* It allowed us to laugh at ourselves. I am grateful today for writers such as Christian Lander (2008, 2010) who brilliantly manage to provide a humorous, tongue-in-cheek approach to taking a look in the mirror at whiteness. I also enjoy the witty and biting work of Michael Harriott in his weekly podcast, *The Black One.* In their hilarious send up of country music's vintage stars, the comedic duo of "Doyle and Debbie," a.k.a Bruce Arntson and Jennie Littleton, manage to both satirize and adore iconic Americana with their wickedly brilliant script and funny original songs.

In looking back at the television show *All in The Family,* I can only marvel at the skill of the show's writers to give us Archie Bunker and his family as a mirror of life in America. Life is hard enough and those who make us laugh are the holy people.

The year following John's passing, I stepped down from a thirty-year career as a development professional in the nonprofit sector. I believe the intention of those thirty years was to comfort the afflicted. My unfolding next chapter seems to be about afflicting the comfortable, starting with myself, and hopefully using my capacity to skillfully relate with people of all ages—children, young adults, older adults—in new and expanded ways. Transformation is the natural process for all of life, all of the time. There is still so much work to be done to dismantle whiteness. My necessary next action steps are as much about freeing myself from the cultural habit of racism as they are about challenging laws and customs. As Nelson Mandela said, "People must learn to hate, and if they can learn to hate, they can be taught to love, for love comes more naturally to the human heart than its opposite . . .

Man's goodness is a flame that can be hidden but never extinguished." (Mandela 1994)

We're all in this together. What white folks will choose to remember and reclaim their humanity and address the visible and invisible racial lines dividing our country? Who will challenge corporations to acknowledge and rectify their central role in exploiting the underclass? Who will redefine white people's place in American culture through civil discourse? I invite you to join those committed to fighting for social and economic justice in saying, "We'll do it."

Carry it on. ■

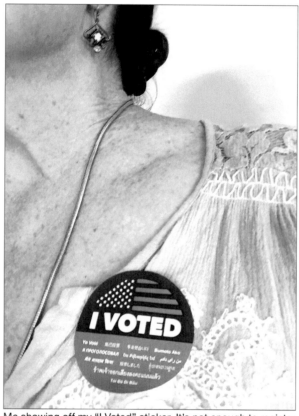

Me showing off my "I Voted" sticker. It's not enough to register and exercise your personal right to vote. Be informed about voter suppression, both legal and illegal. Work to ensure ALL eligible voters can exercise their right to vote. *Carolyn L. Baker Family Archives.*

Some of the books from my local library I read while writing *An Unintentional Accomplice.* See suggested reading titles in the Bibliography. *Carolyn L. Baker Family Archives.*

Here I am with one of my six grandchildren in Malibu, CA, 2017. It's important to share a laugh along the way and enjoy the journey. *Carolyn L. Baker Family Archives.*

AFTERWORD

WE TEND TO LIKE STORIES that have a beginning, a middle, and an end. Since my story began with my childhood growing up in Lakewood, California, revisiting the evolution of both it and myself is where I will close.

The City of Lakewood has celebrated the sixty-fifth anniversary of its 1954 incorporation. There is a website devoted to the story of my hometown (http://www.lakewoodcity.org), and the "Lakewood Plan," the first of its kind contract city. The vintage photos and video stories fill me with nostalgia and gratitude for such a wonderful childhood. This trip down memory lane prompted me to dig out an old newspaper clipping from 1954. The headline reads, "6-Year-Old Boy's Parakeet Wins Top Honors in Lakewood Gardens Pet Parade." The story and photo features my brother John standing in front of a very elaborate, homemade float pulled by his wagon which included his pet parakeet in a cage. John stands in full costume, with a broad smile, as the winner of the Sweepstakes Prize for the most outstanding entry. Those were the days. "No theorist or urban planner had the experience then to gauge how thirty thousand former GI's and their wives would take to frame and stucco houses on small rectangular lots next to hog farms and dairies." (Waldie 1996). My experience tells me we took to the Lakewood experiment with great joy and hope.

In the early 1950s when my family moved in, our Lakewood Gardens neighbors included many Catholics and Jews. I went to Mass at St. Pancratius with my friends and its annual Carnival was beloved by all. It was the scene of many first quasi dates. Halloween meant homemade costumes, imaginatively worked on for weeks, and, repeated the collection of hauls of candy in pillow cases. The family next door, self-identified Okies, handed out hundreds of their famous, handmade popcorn balls each year. The friends I grew up with, in Lakewood Gardens, remain my lifelong best friends. We shared the golden years in Southern California.

The concept of whiteness had, by that time, been expanded to include families such as these. These neighbors may have experienced discrimination of some sort in the past, but here they found a welcome mat. The City of Lakewood matched its East Coast counterpart, Levittown in New York, in ethnic and religious diversity. But similar to Levittown, Lakewood excluded people of color. In the year I was born, 1953, Levittown had become the largest community in the country, at almost 70,000, without a single African American resident (Waldie 1996). In 1960, whites made up nearly 99 percent of Lakewood's population. Out of its 67,125 residents, only seven were black.

As I poured through the amazing sixty-five year history of Lakewood, I realized the account omits the same realities of exclusion that I also hadn't acknowledged until recent times. At its founding, salesmen openly steered African Americans and working class Latinos away from Lakewood toward communities such as Compton. Sales staff refused housing applications submitted by black families. In 1955, civil rights attorney Loren Miller would note that Lakewood had become a bustling, "lily white" metropolis that had been "made white, kept white by builders with the active consent of the Federal Housing Administration (FHA)." (Straus 2014).

This is an important part of the story too. It's abundantly clear that during the mid-twentieth century, rapid creation of thousands of tract homes was an extraordinary feat of vision and engineering. And the Lakewood Plan for contracted services was an innovative game changer. Yet, in parallel, it is equally important to acknowledge the deep influence and impact this social engineering had in shaping my mindset as a white child growing up in segregated Southern California. And how slow the evolution and progress has been —both on my part and that of the culture.

✴ ✴ ✴

As we go to press, covid-19 is raging around the world. In addition to creating cross-sector, worldwide human suffering, the spread of the coronavirus in America is also exposing the vulnerability of a social safety net supposedly designed to aid and protect all Americans from hunger, poverty, and economic hardship. There is strong historical and international evidence showing that social spending programs drastically reduce the health and wealth divide. Yet the United States does less than many other nations to address its inherent inequality through public policy. While the coronavirus is no respecter of socio-economic status, and each and every one of us is profoundly affected, it has also "exposed" the role race and class has played in the systemic mismanagement of the pandemic, in much the same way they did during Hurricane Katrina.

There was a time when Americans, specifically white Americans such as myself, eagerly supported government entitlement programs and had relatively no issue having a social safety net in place. Many of us from the suburbs like to think we got to where we are today by virtue of our merit, hard work, intelligence, pluck, and maybe a little luck. But it was America's investment after World War II that created FHA home programs and later the Veterans Administration (VA), which backed $120 billion of home loans between 1934 and 1962. It insured long term mortgage loans by private lenders for home construction and sale. It allowed for a repayment period of 25-30 years. If the person with the mortgage defaulted, the FHA would indemnify (pay) the bank. Thus there was a loan guarantee for the bank, making it possible for millions of average white Americans, such as my family, to own a home for the first time. Of the 350,000 new homes built with federal support in Northern California between 1946 and 1960, fewer than 100 went to African Americans (Lipsitz 2006).

My family and I were the recipients of life-changing white welfare. This example, along with the creation of public schools, state colleges, and gigantic programs such as rural electrification and assistance from the G.I. Bill, was one of the largest wealth-creation and intergenerational wealth-transfer programs in history. In short, even when we were a much poorer nation, we made huge national investments and made it a priority to help disadvantaged white Americans, while African Americans and other people of color were, for the most part, denied access. Today's extreme racial wealth gap is the most obvious result of the distribution of these entitlements.

Thus, as white American's moved into a burgeoning middle-class, poverty became racialized.

I long remember hearing the phrase, "pull yourself up by your own bootstraps" as part of my sociopolitical upbringing, about self-reliance. Many white people I know evoke the bootstrap phrase when they want to argue against welfare and other social programs, using racist stereotypes such as corrupt, undeserving "welfare queens" who take money from hardworking taxpayers. In their reality, white people are seen as the only hardworking taxpayers in the country. This trope would also suggest these benefit programs are counterproductive in that they foster "dependency." This might have been a plausible argument a generation ago, but the evidence now indicates this is incorrect. The resulting safety net cutbacks, due to this bootstrap policy, has made it especially hard for low-income individuals to access food stamps and health benefits, and has diminished our social safety net.

Strikingly, about 13 million white people living in poverty are in dire need of help, but are so antagonistic about benefits programs they would share with people of color that they refuse to apply for government assistance.[1] In my own case, perhaps the most alarming aspect of this way of thinking was my lack of empathy across racial and economic lines. So now, a pandemic that will surely change our manner of living is successfully highlighting our underlying U.S. social and economic disparities.

---

1.   Tracy Jan, "13 million people in poverty are disconnected from the social safety net. Most of them are white."*The Washington Post*, February 4, 2019. https://www.washingtonpost.com/business/economy/13-million-people-in-poverty-are-disconnected-from-the-social-safety-net-most-of-them-are-white/2019/02/04/807516a0-2598-11e9-81fd-b7b05d5bed90_story.html.

Right now, the COVID-19 crisis is affecting the working class, low-wage, and the poor the worst, many of whom aren't paid if they miss work and are least able to afford it. According to a 2019 Federal Reserve study, 40 percent of Americans could not come up with $400 to cover an emergency.[2] Given the occupational segregation in this country, when I think of these low-wage workers they're more likely to be women, immigrants, black and Latino workers. This pandemic will certainly hit some communities harder than others. COVID-19 may help us understand the depth of the racial and class divide in American society. We must take a heartfelt look at how to build an America that includes everyone. We also need a sweeping examination of how racism and classism has broken the country's social compact, and stunted the development of nearly every institution crucial for a healthy society. This includes organized labor, public education, wage and hour standards, job-based health and retirement security, as well as our social safety net, which should be available for all Americans, regardless of race, class, or ethnicity.

✳ ✳ ✳

TODAY, THE CITY OF LAKEWOOD is no longer a Whitopia —only about half of its citizens are white. A growing mix of Latino, Asian, and black residents creates rich racial diversity. Its motto "Tomorrow's City Today" has evolved to "Times Change. Values Don't." Indeed, I can see the cherished values of my childhood such as youth sports programs, public parks, and volunteerism are still alive and

2. "Report on the Economic Well-Being of U.S. Households in 2018, Dealing with Unexpected Expenses," May 2019. https://www.federalreserve.gov/publications/2019-economic-well-being-of-us-households-in-2018-dealing-with-unexpected-expenses.htm.

well in the City of Lakewood. My hometown continues to represent me in many ways. There is more to be done to acknowledge the past, and it is a work in progress.

Lakewood's shift from white entitlement towards equality and inclusion corresponds with my own. There is an old Girl Scout song, "Make New Friends" often sung as a round. It speaks of the importance of not forgetting the past as we move and grow. In like manner, I hope my own evolution contributes to embracing and telling the full story. It is within that vulnerability our strength and healing lies. ■

In Loving Memory of John Hillis Baker
(1947-2017)

Carolyn L. Baker Family Archives.

ANTI-RACIST CHECKLIST

HERE ARE SOME of the real-life ways an ordinary white person can do something extraordinary — take responsibility for a political vision in which all are equal in the eyes of the law:

☐ When a person of color is being discriminated against, don't be indifferent.

☐ Speak up on behalf of those who have it less comfortable than me within my sphere, right where I am — my neighborhood, my office, my place of prayer, my street, where I shop.

☐ Examine to what degree my lifestyle inflicts damage and contributes to poverty on the labor of others.

☐ Be willing to see myself as less tremendous and more human.

☐ Work to see the blind spots, the unconscious daily racial biases still buried within my psyche.

☐ Meaningfully and regularly interact with races, ethnicities, ages, orientations, genders, abilities, political views, and faiths other than my own. Talk to others with an open mind, rather than a fixed position. Better yet, stop talking and listen.

- ☐ Put my God-given abilities to work in service to the whole, rather than self-advancement.

- ☐ Become a "Legal Observer," and volunteer as an elections worker.

- ☐ If a white person attacks or demands a black person to defend #BlackLivesMatter, direct that conversation to myself for further discussion.

- ☐ Be an accountable ally to people of color.

- ☐ Take responsibility for the journey of my racial identity.

- ☐ Notice ways in which white privilege makes me free from race-based humiliation and suspicion.

- ☐ Knowing the truth about black history and the racial justice movement by reading books by black authors.

- ☐ Love America by looking at it in the face.

- ☐ Nurture a positive anti-racist white identity within my family and honor the heritage of white anti-racist resistors.

- ☐ Host a community forum, a discussion salon, concerning what white privilege, anti-blackness, patriarchy, and other oppressions are — and how to address them in everyday life. Commit to no longer ignoring and being silent on these issues.

- ☐ Speak with clergy about ways the church, through its silence, is perpetuating racism and structures limiting equal access to democracy, justice, education, and the economy. Ask the leaders to redouble their commitment to being instruments of peace, and evidencing it.

- Donate when I can to those individuals and organizations that advance civilization concerning race and class issues.

- Call, tweet, email, and/or write my elected officials and weigh in on civil rights issues. The Capital switchboard number is (202) 224-3121. The contact info for US Senators; US House of Representatives Congresspersons; State Governors; State Senators; State Assemblypersons; County Supervisors; and City Councilpersons is easily available online.

- Participate in a Living Legacy Pilgrimage, an experiential learning opportunity to deepen understanding of the Civil Rights Movement by visiting the sites where it happened and talking with the people who lived it. www.uulivinglegacy.org

- Download and read the free material on Civic Online Reasoning (COR) from the Stanford Historical Education Group www.cor.sanford.edu.

- Discover twenty two conversation techniques that serve to complicate the narrative at the Solutions Journalism Network, follow them @soljourno, and visit www.solutionsjournalism.org.

These practices may constitute new habits. And maybe it's as simple as is said in 12-step programs, "Fake it till you make it" Why do this? After all, why would someone with privilege want to give it up? Because it's the right and decent thing to do. It's the right thing for myself, for my family, for my grandchildren's future, and for the community in which I live. If I'm lucky, I've got maybe twenty years left on the planet. I want it to stand for something. ∎

Acknowledgments

A LIST OF ALL THOSE who have, in one way or another, contributed to this book would spill over into numerous pages, so I collectively express my heartfelt thanks to everyone who has, in their unique ways, added to publishing this book. I especially and gratefully acknowledge and give credit to each of the authors listed in the Bibliography. Their clarity and insight were a significant source of my increased understanding and commitment. I hope my perspective amplifies their essential work. Any and all kudos for this book go to the 2Leaf Press, whose mission it is to foster understanding of and respect for cultural diversity through literature and media literacy. In particular, my deepest gratitude and admiration goes to its publisher, Gabrielle David, who took an early interest in the project and gave it a chance. Gabrielle's unflagging dedication to the power of the written word was a constant inspiration as she motivated me to dig deeper; and to Kathryn Siddell for the skillful copyediting. To each and every one of my family and friends who encouraged me to keep writing, I thank you for the sincere support and faith in this labor of love. And I would be remiss in not acknowledging the powers that be, guiding my life each step of the way. As I'm fond of saying as I gaze skyward, "Thanks Everybody!"■

Bibliography

Andersen, Michelle. *The New Jim Crow: Mass Incarceration in the Age of Colorblindness.* New York: The New Press, 2012.

Anderson, Carol. *White Rage: The Unspoken Truth of Our Racial Divide.* London, UK: Bloomsbury Publishing, 2016.

Anderson, Carol. "Ferguson isn't about black rage against cops. It's white rage against progress." *The Washington Post.* August 29, 2014. https://www.washingtonpost.com/opinions/ferguson-wasnt-black-rage-against-copsit-was-white-rage-against-progress/2014/08/29/3055e3f4-2d75-11e4-bb9b-997ae-96fad33_story.html.

Baldwin, James. *The Fire Next Time.* New York: Dial Press, 1963.

Benjamin, Rich. *Searching for Whitopia: An Improbable Journey to the Heart of White America.* New York: Hyperion, 2009.

Blackwell, Kelsey. "Why People of Color Need Spaces Without White People." *The Arrow: A Journal of Wakeful Society, Culture, and Politics.* August 2018.

Blee, Kathleen M. *Women of the Klan: Racism and Gender in the 1920s.* Los Angeles: University of California Press, 2008.

Callaghan, Barry "An Interview with Angela Davis in a California Prison," Canada: 1971.

Cameron, Julia. *The Artist's Way: A Spiritual Path to Higher Creativity.* New York: Tarcher Putnam, 1992.

Crenshaw, Kimberle. "Why Intersectionality Can't Wait." *The Washington Post: In Theory.* September 24, 2015. https://www.washingtonpost.com/news/in-theory/wp/2015/09/24/why-intersectionality-cant-wait.

Cleaver, Eldridge. *Soul on Ice.* Delta, 1968.

Coates, Ta-Nehisi. *Between the World and Me.* New York: Speigel & Grau, Penguin Random House, 2015.

Coleman, Peter T. *The Five Percent: Finding solutions to seemingly impossible conflicts.* New York: Public Affairs, Perseus Books Group, 2011.

Collins, Patricia Hill. *Black Feminist Thought.* Routledge Classics, 2008.

Cox, Karen L. *Dixie's Daughters: The United Daughters of the Confederacy and the Preservation of Confederate Culture.* Florida: University Press of Florida, 2003.

Dass, Ram. *Be Here Now.* New York: Harmony Books, 1971.

David, Gabrielle. *TRAILBLAZERS: Black Women Who Helped Make America Great.* New York: 2LeafPress, 2020.

David, Gabrielle and Sean Frederick Forbes. *What Does it Mean to be White in America?: Breaking the White Code of Silence, A Collection of Personal Narratives.* New York: 2LeafPress, 2016.

Davis, Townsend. Weary Feet, Rested Souls: A Guided History of the Civil Rights Movement. New York, New York: W.W. Norton & Company, 1998. DeGruy, Joy. *Post Traumatic Slave Syndrome.* Uptone Press, 2017.

Demetrakas, Johanna, dir. *Feminists: What Were They Thinking?* 2018; Netflix.

Diehl, Paul and Gary Goertz. *War and Peace in International Rivalry.* University of Michigan Press, 2000.

Du Bois, W.E.B. *The Souls of Black Folk.* Dover Publications, 1994.

Dyson, Michael Eric. *Tears We Cannot Stop: A Sermon to White America.* New York: St. Martin's Press, 2017.

Emba, Christine. "Intersectionality." *The Washington Post: In Theory.* September 21, 2015. https://www.washingtonpost.com/news/in-theory/wp/2015/09/21/intersectionality-a-primer/

Feagin, Joe R. *The White Racial Frame: Centuries of Racial Framing and Counter-Framing.* New York: Routledge, 2013.

Feagin, Joe R. and Eileen O'Brien. *White Men on Race: Power, Privilege, and the Shaping of Cultural Consciousness.* Boston: Beacon Press, 2003.

Francis, John. *Planetwalker: A Memoir of 22 Years of Walking and 17 Years of Silence.* National Geographic Society. April, 2008.

Griffin, Paul R. *Seeds of Racism in the Soul of America.* Naperville, Illinois: Sourcebooks, Inc., 2000.

Harvey, Jennifer and Tim Wise. *Raising White Kids: Bringing Up Children in a Racially Unjust America.* Nashville: Abingdon Press, 2018.

Irving, Debby. *Waking Up White, and Finding Myself in the Story of Race.* Elephant Room Press, 2014.

Isenberg, Nancy. *White Trash: The 400-Year Untold History of Class in America.* New York: Viking, 2016.

Johnson, Theodore. "Overcoming Racism through National Solidarity." Brennan Center for Justice, December 7, 2018. https://www.brennancenter.org/our-work/analysis-opinion/overcoming-racism-through-national-solidarity.

Kahn, Yasmin Sabina. *Enlightening the World: The Creation of the Statue of Liberty.* New York: Cornell University Press, 2010.

Kimmel, Michael S. and Abby L. Ferber. *Privilege: A Reader.* Boulder, CO: Westview Press, 2003.

King Jr., Martin Luther. "The Montgomery Bus Boycott." Speech delivered at the Holt Street Baptist Church, Montgomery, AL, December 5, 1955. Stanford: The Martin Luther King, Jr. Research and Education Institute. https://kinginstitute.stanford.edu/encyclopedia/montgomery-bus-boycott.

King Jr., Martin Luther. "Remaining Awake Through a Great Revolution." Speech delivered at the National Cathedral, Washington, D.C., March 31, 1968. Stanford: The Martin Luther King, Jr. Research and Education Institute. https://kinginstitute.stanford.edu/king-papers/publications/knock-midnight-inspiration-great-sermons-reverend-martin-luther-king-jr-10.

Lander, Christian. *Stuff White People Like: The Definitive Guide to the Unique Taste of Millions.* New York: Random House, 2008.

Lander, Christian. *Whiter Shades of Pale: The Stuff White People Like, Coast to Coast from Seattle's Sweaters to Maine's Microbrews.* New York: Random House, 2010.

Levinson, Sanford. *Our Undemocratic Constitution: Where the Constitution Goes Wrong (And How We the People Can Correct It).* New York: Oxford University Press, 2008.

Lipsitz, George. *The Possessive Investment in Whiteness.* Philadelphia, PA: Temple University Press, 2006.

Lorde, Audre. *Sister Outsider: Essays and Speeches.* Canada: Crossing Press, 2007.

MacIntosh, Peggy. "White Privilege and Male Privilege: A Personal Account of Coming To See Correspondences through Work in Women's Studies." *Peace and Freedom Magazine,* (July/August, 1989): 10-12.

Mandela, Nelson. *Long Walk to Freedom.* New York: Little Brown & Co., 1994.

McRae, Elisabeth Gillespie. *Mothers of Massive Resistance: White Women and the Politics of White Supremacy.* New York: Oxford University Press, 2018.

Miller, Caroline Adams. *Getting Grit: The Evidence-Based Approach to Cultivating Passion, Perseverance, and Purpose.* Louisville, CO: Sounds True, 2017.

Morrison, Toni. *Playing in the Dark: Whiteness and the Literary Imagination.* New York: Vintage, 1993.

Moyo, Dambisa. *Dead Aid: Why Aid is not Working and How there is a Better Way for Africa.* New York: Penguin, 2009.

Olou, Ijeoma. *So You Want to Talk About Race.* New York: Seal Press, 2019.

Olson, Gary. *Empathy Imperiled: Capitalism, Culture and the Brain.* New York: Springer, 2013.

Painter, Nell Irving. *The History of White People.* New York: W.W. Norton & Company, 2011.

Pearce, Joseph Chilton. *The Crack in the Cosmic Egg.* Maine: Park Street Press, 2002.

Pilgrim, Peace. *Her Life and Work in Her Own Words.* Santa Fe, New Mexico: Ocean Tree Books, 1992.

Pollan, Michael. *How to Change Your Mind: What New Science of Psychedelics Teaches Us About Consciousness, Dying, Addiction, Depression, and Transcendence.* New York: Penguin Press, 2018.

Rampersad, Arnold, ed. *The Collected Poems of Langston Hughes.* New York: Vintage, 1995.

Rankine, Claudia. *Citizen, An American Lyric.* Minnesota: Graywolf Press, 2014.

Reich, Robert B. *Saving Capitalism for the Many, Not the Few. Beyond Outrage.* New York: Vintage, 2016.

Reich, Robert B. *The Common Good.* New York: Vintage, 2019.

Robinson, Randall. *The Debt: What America Owes to Blacks.* New York: Plume, 2001.

Sawyer, Wendy. "Youth Confinement: The Whole Pie 2019." Prison Policy Initiative. December 19, 2019. https://www.prisonpolicy.org/reports/youth2019.html.

Schumacher, E. F. *Small is Beautiful: Economics as if People Mattered.* New York: Harper, 1973.

Smith, Clint. *Counting Descent.* Los Angeles: Write Bloody Publishing, 2016.

Spruill, Marjorie J. *Divided We Stand: The Battle Over Woman's Rights and Family Values That Polarized American Politics.* New York: Bloomsbury Publishing, 2017.

Stiles, Matt. "LA County juvenile halls are so chaotic, offices are afraid to go to work." *Los Angeles Times,* May 19, 2018. https://www.latimes.com/local/countygovernment/la-me-juvenile-halls-chaos-pepper-spray-detention-probation-20190519-story.html.

Strauss, Emily E. *Death of a Suburban Dream: Race and Schools in Compton, California.* Philadelphia, PA: University of Pennsylvania Press, 2014.

Till, Mamie, and Christopher Benson. *Death of Innocence: The Story of the Hate Crime that Changed America.* London, UK: Oneworld Publications, 2004.

Tyson, Timothy B. *The Blood of Emmett Till.* New York: Simon & Schuster, 2017.

Waldie, Donald J. *Holy Land: A Suburban Memoir.* New York: W.W. Norton & Company, 1996.

Walker, Alice. *In Search of Our Mothers' Gardens: Womanist Prose.* Boston, MA: Mariner Books, 2003.

Watts, Alan. *The Book: On the Taboo Against Knowing Who You Are.* New York: Vintage Books 1989.

Williams, J. Patricia. *The Alchemy of Race and Rights. Alchemy of Race and Rights: Diary of a Law Professor.* Boston, MA: Harvard University Press, 1992.

Wise, Tim J. *Affirmative Action: Racial Preference in Black and White (Positions: Education, Politics, and Culture).* New York: Routledge, 2012.

Wise, Tim. *Between Barack and a Hard Place: Racism and White Denial in the Age of Obama.* San Francisco: City Light Publishers, 2009.

Wise, Tim. *Colorblind: The Rise of Post-Racial Politics and the Retreat from Racial Equity.* San Francisco: City Light Publishers, 2010.

Wise, Tim. *Culture of Cruelty: How America's Elite Demonize the Poor, Valorize the Rich and Jeopardize the Future.* San Francisco: City Lights Publishers, 2014.

Wise, Tim. *Dear White America: Letter to a New Minority.* San Francisco: City Light Publishers, 2012.

Wise, Tim. *Speaking Treason Fluently: Anti-Racist Reflections From an Angry White Male.* San Francisco: City Light Publishers, 2008.

Wise, Tim. *Under the Affluence: Shaming the Poor, Praising the Rich and Sacrificing the Future of America.* San Francisco: City Light Publishers, 2015.

Wise, Tim. *White Like Me: Reflections on Race from a Privileged Son.* San Francisco: City Light Publishers, 2005.

ABOUT THE AUTHOR

CAROLYN L. BAKER has spent decades working and investing in her native Los Angeles as a senior executive in the nonprofit sector. Formerly an adjunct professor in the community college systems, Baker earned a graduate degree in Organizational Development from Northern Arizona University and began a thirty year executive career in nonprofit settings as wide-ranging as Skid Row in downtown Los Angeles, to the West Los Angeles Veterans Campus, to the Clinton Global Initiative. As a development professional, Baker has directed capital campaigns, annual solicitations, and proposals to private and governmental funders raising millions of dollars for safety net causes. *An Unintentional Accomplice: A Personal Perspective on White Responsibility* is her first book. ∎

OTHER BOOKS BY 2LEAF PRESS

2LEAF PRESS challenges the status quo by publishing alternative fiction, non-fiction, poetry and bilingual works by activists, academics, poets and authors dedicated to diversity and social justice with scholarship that is accessible to the general public. 2LEAF PRESS produces high quality and beautifully produced hardcover, paperback and ebook formats through our series: *2LP Explorations in Diversity, 2LP University Books, 2LP Classics, 2LP Translations, Nuyorican World Series,* and *2LP Current Affairs, Culture & Politics.* Below is a selection of 2LEAF PRESS' published titles.

2LP EXPLORATIONS IN DIVERSITY

Substance of Fire: Gender and Race in the College Classroom
by Claire Millikin
Foreword by R. Joseph Rodríguez, Afterword by Richard Delgado
Contributed material by Riley Blanks, Blake Calhoun, Rox Trujillo

Black Lives Have Always Mattered
A Collection of Essays, Poems, and Personal Narratives
Edited by Abiodun Oyewole

The Beiging of America:
Personal Narratives about Being Mixed Race in the 21st Century
Edited by Cathy J. Schlund-Vials, Sean Frederick Forbes, Tara Betts
with an Afterword by Heidi Durrow

What Does it Mean to be White in America?
Breaking the White Code of Silence, A Collection of Personal Narratives
Edited by Gabrielle David and Sean Frederick Forbes
Introduction by Debby Irving and Afterword by Tara Betts

2LP CLASSICS

Adventures in Black and White
Edited and with a critical introduction by Tara Betts
by Philippa Duke Schuyler

Monsters: Mary Shelley's Frankenstein and Mathilda
by Mary Shelley, edited by Claire Millikin Raymond

2LP TRANSLATIONS

Birds on the Kiswar Tree
by Odi Gonzales, Translated by Lynn Levin
Bilingual: English/Spanish

Incessant Beauty, A Bilingual Anthology
by Ana Rossetti, Edited and Translated by Carmela Ferradáns
Bilingual: English/Spanish

NUYORICAN WORLD SERIES

Our Nuyorican Thing, The Birth of a Self-Made Identity
by Samuel Carrion Diaz, with an Introduction by Urayoán Noel
Bilingual: English/Spanish

Hey Yo! Yo Soy!, 40 Years of Nuyorican Street Poetry,
The Collected Works of Jesús Papoleto Meléndez
Bilingual: English/Spanish

LITERARY NONFICTION

No Vacancy; Homeless Women in Paradise
by Michael Reid

The Beauty of Being, A Collection of Fables, Short Stories & Essays
by Abiodun Oyewole

WHEREABOUTS: Stepping Out of Place,
An Outside in Literary & Travel Magazine Anthology
Edited by Brandi Dawn Henderson

PLAYS

Rivers of Women, The Play
by Shirley Bradley LeFlore, with photographs by Michael J. Bracey